# Real-Life Math
## ALGEBRA

**SECOND EDITION**

WALCH PUBLISHING

1    2    3    4    5    6    7    8    9    10

ISBN 978-0-8251-6324-1

Copyright © 1998, 2007

J. Weston Walch, Publisher

P. O. Box 658 • Portland, Maine 04104-0658

www.walch.com

Printed in the United States of America

**WALCH** **PUBLISHING**

# Table of Contents

## Literal Equations—Formulas

## Ratios, Proportions, and Percents

## Data and Graphs

## Systems of Equations I

## Systems of Equations II

# Table of Contents

# How to Use This Series

The *Real-Life Math* series is a collection of activities designed to put math into the context of real-world settings. This series contains math appropriate for pre-algebra students all the way up to pre-calculus students. Problems can be used as reminders of old skills in new contexts, as an opportunity to show how a particular skill is used, or as an enrichment activity for stronger students. Because this is a collection of reproducible activities, you may make as many copies of each activity as you wish.

Please be aware that this collection does not and cannot replace teacher supervision. Although formulas are often given on the student page, this does not replace teacher instruction on the subjects to be covered. Teaching notes include extension suggestions, some of which may involve the use of outside experts. If it is not possible to get these presenters to come to your classroom, it may be desirable to have individual students contact them.

We have found a significant number of real-world settings for this collection, but it is not a complete list. Let your imagination go, and use your own experience or the experience of your students to create similar opportunities for contextual study.

# Introduction

## Organization

The book is organized around four themes of interest to students: Sports, Money, Science/Technology, and Travel/Transportation. There are eight topics addressing key algebraic concepts: Literal Equations—Formulas; Ratios, Proportions, and Percents; Data and Graphs; Systems of Equations I and II; Quadratics; Nonlinear Functions; and Miscellaneous topics. There are four activities for each of the eight topics, making a total of 32 student activities.

## NCTM Standards

The activities address many of the NCTM standards for grades 9 through 12: algebra, data analysis and probability, problem solving, communication, connections, and representation.

## Order of Activities and Time Considerations

The activities are arranged to reflect the order in which algebraic concepts are presented in many textbooks. You can use this resource to enrich a concept presented in your textbook or use the activities as an introduction to a new concept. The activities can be done in any order; however, before students start the Systems of Equations activities, they should have some facility with the concepts presented in the first part of the book.

Because students' ability levels and schools' schedules vary greatly, time suggestions for the activities are not given. Prior to using an activity, review it and decide how much time would be appropriate for your students.

## Level of Difficulty

Some activities use more difficult algebraic concepts than others. As a general rule, the activities in the second half of the book are more difficult than those in the first half. The lessons that are less difficult mathematically still involve higher-order thinking skills.

## Graphing Calculators and Other Technology

Students should have access to graphing calculators. However, keep in mind that many students have difficulty choosing appropriate settings (e.g., intervals for the $x$ and $y$ axes) for their graphs. Review with them how to choose correct settings prior to using the activities. In addition, many of the lessons ask students to build tables, find lines and curves of best fit, and perform linear, quadratic, and exponential regressions. You may want to review these functions on your specific model of graphing calculator prior to using the activities with your students. It's always tricky to know whether to allow students to construct graphs by hand first and then use their graphing calculators, or to let them use the graphing calculator right from the start. Experiment, and decide which method works best. In some of the activities, students can use spreadsheet, word processing, graphing, and desktop publishing software.

# 1. The Grass Is Greener

## Context

sports

## Topic

literal equations—formulas

## Overview

In this activity, students assume the role of a baseball coach and must devise and carry out a plan to determine how much sod they will need to cover the baseball field.

## Objectives

Students will be able to:

- devise and carry out a plan to find the area of an irregular shape

## Materials

- one copy of the Activity 1 handout for each student

- tape measure or trundle wheel, one per group

- graph paper

- access to a baseball field

## Teaching Notes

- Students can work with a partner or in small groups for this activity.

- There are many different ways of determining the area of an irregular shape. Some possible strategies include measuring the field and making a scale drawing; dividing the field into common geometric shapes; and treating the entire field as a single geometric figure (such as a triangle or sector of a circle), then subtracting the area of the infield dirt.

- Review students' plans prior to having them measure the baseball field.

## Answers

Answers will vary depending on the size of the baseball field at your school.

## Extension Activities

- Students can apply different strategies and decide which is most accurate.

- Ask students to think of other instances in which they might want to find the area of an irregular shape.

# 1. The Grass Is Greener

Imagine you are a baseball coach at a large high school. You are about to write a memo to the athletic director (AD) requesting funding to resod the baseball field. Because the Athletic Department's budget is always very tight, you know that the AD will ask you to carefully document the costs that you submit. Devise and carry out a plan to calculate how much sod you will need for the baseball field. Use the baseball field at your school as a model for making the plan.

**Sod Information**

- One roll of sod covers 40 square yards.

- The price per roll is $98.

**Make a Plan**

1. Consult with the other members of your group. Devise a strategy to determine the amount of sod you will need for the baseball field. The formulas below may prove useful ($b$ = base; $h$ = height; $s$ = side; $r$ = radius; $N$ = a central angle measuring $N°$).

    area of a triangle: $\frac{1}{2} bh$      area of a trapezoid: $\frac{1}{2} h(b_1 + b_2)$

    area of a rectangle: $bh$      area of a circle: $\pi^2$

    area of a square: $s^2$      area of a sector: $\dfrac{N}{360} \pi r^2$

2. On a separate sheet of paper, describe your plan for measuring the baseball field. Then have your teacher approve the plan.

3. Carry out your plan and measure the baseball field.

4. Review the plan you gave to the teacher. Describe any modifications you had to make to your original plan after you started measuring.

5. What are the dimensions of the baseball field?

6. How many square feet of sod will you need?

7. How many rolls of sod will you request?

8. What is the total cost of the sod?

9. On a separate sheet of paper, draft a memo to the athletic director stating your request. Include an enclosure showing how you arrived at your cost.

# 2. My First Car

## Context

money

## Topic

literal equations—formulas

## Overview

In this activity, students calculate monthly payments for cars they would like to buy.

## Objectives

Students will be able to:

- calculate monthly payments using a formula

- evaluate the impact on monthly payments as parameters change

## Materials

- one copy of the Activity 2 handout for each student

- classified ads or publications selling cars

- computers with spreadsheet program (optional)

## Teaching Notes

- Students can work individually, with a partner, or in small groups for this activity.

- Model using the formula for calculating monthly payments prior to having students use it. You may wish to suggest that students use a spreadsheet for the formula.

- Remind students to change annual percentage rates from percentages to decimals, and point out to them that $n$ is the number of months—not years—of the loan.

- Students could also use online car ads if they have access to the Internet.

## Answers

Answers will vary depending on cars selected.

## Extension Activity

Students can investigate other loan types and calculate monthly loan payments.

# 2. My First Car

Deciding what type of car to buy is a big decision. Unless you can pay cash for a car, the decision can be made for you by how much you can afford to pay each month. If you borrow money, the amount you pay each month depends on how much you borrow, for how long, and at what interest rate. Work through the questions below to find out how monthly payments change depending on the amount of the loan, the interest rate, and the length of the loan.

The formula for calculating the monthly payment of a loan is given below.

$$m = \frac{A(\frac{r}{12})(1+\frac{r}{12})^n}{(1+\frac{r}{12})^n - 1}$$

In the formula, $m$ = the monthly payment, $A$ = the amount of the loan, $r$ = the annual interest rate (expressed as a decimal), and $n$ = the number of months of the loan.

1. Look through the classified ads section of the newspaper or other publication and choose three different cars to buy. List the three cars and their prices below.

### Cars and Prices

| Car name | | | |
|----------|---|---|---|
| Price | | | |

2. Use the formula listed above to calculate the monthly payment of the cars you have selected. In this case, let $n$ = 48 months (4 years) and $r$ = 8.25%. List the monthly payments in the table.

### Monthly Payments on a 4-Year Loan

| Car name | | | |
|----------|---|---|---|
| Monthly payment | | | |

*(continued)*

# 2. My First Car

3. Generally, loans for longer periods of time have lower interest rates than loans for shorter periods of time. Predict how the monthly payments will change if the length of the loan is extended to 5 years and the annual interest rate is reduced to 8%.

4. Calculate the monthly loan amounts based on a 5-year loan and an 8% annual interest rate. List the results in the table below.

### Monthly Payments on a 5-Year Loan

| Car name | | | |
|---|---|---|---|
| Monthly payment | | | |

5. How accurate were your predictions from question 3?

6. Which factor do you suppose has the greatest effect on the amount of the monthly payment—interest rates or the length of a loan? Explain your reasoning.

7. Explain which is a better loan: a longer period of time at a lower interest rate, or a shorter period of time at a higher interest rate.

# 3. Energy Savings

## Context

science/technology

## Topic

literal equations—formulas

## Overview

In this activity, students calculate the energy costs associated with lighting their school.

## Objectives

Students will be able to:

- calculate energy costs for lighting using a formula

## Materials

- one copy of the Activity 3 handout for each student

- detailed information about the wattage of lights in the school

## Teaching Notes

- Students can work with a partner or in small groups for this activity.

- It is not necessary to have students walk through every classroom and building at your school. Instead, you might want to make data-gathering a class project. Assign teams specific areas (such as the cafeteria or the gym) and have each team share its findings with the whole class.

- Depending on available time and the size of your school, you can modify the lesson by figuring lighting costs for just one classroom or for a portion of the school.

- Review with students how to use a frequency table prior to using the activity.

- If the school uses bulbs of different wattages for similar light types, have students average or estimate the wattage for that category of bulb.

## Answers

Answers will vary depending on the size of and the number of lights at your school.

## Extension Activity

Students can use a similar strategy to calculate the energy costs for lighting their homes.

# 3. Energy Savings

Most people agree that we all need to do our part in conserving natural resources. Have you ever wondered how much your school spends to light the classrooms each year? Work through the steps below to calculate the cost of lighting your school.

1.  Find out how many and what types of lights are used in your school. Count the number of lightbulbs. Keep track of the total using the frequency table below.

### Number of Lights in the School

| Type of light | Watts | Tally | Frequency |
|---|---|---|---|
| fluorescent | | | |
| incandescent | | | |
| halogen | | | |
| mercury vapor | | | |

2.  To calculate the cost of operating the lights at your school, estimate how many hours per day the lights are on, and find out how many days per year the school is in operation.

    number of hours per day: _____

    number of days per year: _____

3.  Calculate the total amount of time the lights are used each year.

    total amount of time: _____

4.  The energy is measured in kilowatt-hours (kWh). Energy usage equals the power times the hours of operation. Use the formula below to calculate the kWh of energy used, where $n$ = the total number of a particular type of lightbulb, $w$ = wattage, and $t$ = time in use in hours. You will need to make a separate calculation for each different type and wattage of bulb.

$$\text{Energy} = nwt\left(\frac{1\text{kw}}{1000\text{w}}\right)$$

**Example:** If you had one hundred 60-watt incandescent bulbs that were in operation for 2080 hours per year, then

$$\text{Energy} = nwt = 100 \times 60 \text{ watts} \times 2080 \text{ hours} \times \frac{1\text{kw}}{1000\text{w}} = 12{,}480 \text{ kWh}$$

Use the table on the next page to record your results.

*(continued)*

# 3. Energy Savings

## Energy Used per Year by Light Type

| Type of light | Energy used |
|---|---|
| fluorescent | |
| incandescent | |
| halogen | |
| mercury vapor | |

5. Calculate the cost of using each light by multiplying the energy used (kWh) by the cost per kWh. Find out what the kWh charge is, or use a figure around 8 cents per kWh.

$$\text{cost per year} = \text{energy used (kWh)} \times \text{cost per kWh}$$

## Cost per Light Type per Year

| Type of light | Fluorescent | Incandescent | Halogen | Mercury vapor |
|---|---|---|---|---|
| Cost per year | | | | |

6. What is the total cost per year for lighting the school?

   total cost per year: _____

7. Based on your lighting investigation, what are some ways the school could reduce its lighting costs?

# 4. What Is the Temperature?

## Context

travel/transportation

## Topic

literal equations—formulas

## Overview

In this activity, students invent their own formula for converting temperature from Celsius to Fahrenheit.

## Objectives

Students will be able to:

- invent an accurate and easy-to-use formula for converting temperature from Celsius to Fahrenheit

## Materials

- one copy of the Activity 4 handout for each student

## Teaching Notes

- Students should invent their new formula individually. They can then work with a partner or group of students when they are ready to share their formulas.

- As an introduction to the activity, ask students if they know what 22 degrees Celsius is in degrees Fahrenheit. Then ask if anyone can tell you what the formula is for making the conversion.

## Answers

Answers will vary, but expect some similarities in the students' formulas, such as changing $\frac{9}{5}$ to 2 and 32 to 30.

## Extension Activity

Students can invent a formula to convert temperature from Fahrenheit to Celsius.

# 4. What Is the Temperature?

At this point in your math career, you have probably used a formula for converting temperature from degrees Celsius to degrees Fahrenheit, but you probably cannot remember the formula off the top of your head. Well, perhaps your memory isn't that bad; maybe the conversion formula is just not very user-friendly. Work through the questions below to develop a user-friendly formula for converting temperature from Celsius to Fahrenheit.

The formula for converting Celsius to Fahrenheit is: $F = \frac{9}{5}C + 32$.

1. Look at the first term in the formula, $\frac{9}{5}C$. How could you change that term to make it easier to work with but still fairly accurate?

2. Look at the second term in the formula, 32. How could you change that term to make it easier to work with but still fairly accurate?

3. Review the ideas you came up with in questions 1 and 2. Combine your two best ideas into one formula.

4. Check the accuracy and the ease of use of your formula by making some temperature conversions and comparing them to results using the original formula. List your findings in the following table.

### Temperature Comparison Chart

| Degrees Celsius | $F = \frac{9}{5}C + 32$ | Your formula for F | Difference |
|---|---|---|---|
| 15° | | | |
| 20° | | | |
| 25° | | | |
| 30° | | | |

*Real-Life Math: Algebra*

# 5.  How Much Can I Eat?

## Context

sports

## Topic

ratios, proportions, and percents

## Overview

In this activity, students use proportions to calculate their daily calorie and nutritional requirements.

## Objectives

Students will be able to:

- set up and solve problems using proportions

## Materials

- one copy of the Activity 5 handout for each student

## Teaching Notes

- Students can work individually, with a partner, or in a small group for this activity.

- Prior to the lesson, have students collect a variety of food labels, excluding soda cans (which don't contain significant nutritional information).

- Introduce the activity by having students decide if they ingest more than 2000 calories per day.

- Stress that the daily calorie requirements are based on averages and may not accurately reflect the students' actual calorie requirements. However, the figures should be accurate enough for the purposes of this activity.

- Values for other age groups are: males 25–50, 174 pounds, 2600 calories; females 25–50, 138 pounds, 2200 calories.

- Explain to students that the calorie amounts given in the table would allow them to maintain their current weight.

- Some students may be sensitive about their weight. If so, you could assign a weight to each student.

## Answers

Answers will vary depending on students' weights and ages.

## Extension Activity

Students can keep track of how many calories they actually ingest in a day and compare those totals with the figures they came up with in the activity.

# 5. How Much Can I Eat?

The nutritional information on a food label doesn't apply to everyone. In fact, the nutritional values listed are for a person who ingests 2000 calories per day, which is appropriate for an 18-year-old female. Create a nutritional table that represents your age and calorie requirements. Work through the steps below to make a profile that fits you.

1.  Use the information in the table below to determine your daily calorie requirements. The amounts listed in the table estimate the number of calories needed to maintain current body weight. Factors such as activity level, height, and body type influence your actual daily calorie requirements.

    **Example:** If you are a 15-year-old male who weighs 160 pounds, then your approximate daily calorie requirements are the following:

    $$\frac{145}{3000} = \frac{160}{x} \qquad x = 3310 \text{ calories per day}$$

    ### Daily Calorie Requirements

| Age | Weight (lbs.) | Calories |
|---|---|---|
| males 11–14 | 99 | 2600 |
| 15–18 | 145 | 3000 |
| 19–24 | 160 | 2800 |
| females 11–14 | 101 | 2000 |
| 15–18 | 120 | 2000 |
| 19–24 | 128 | 2200 |

Source: MyPyramid Plan, USDA, 2005

Your approximate daily calorie requirements: _____

2.  Look over the food labels you collected. You will notice that the nutritional information is listed as "percent daily values based on a 2000 calorie diet." As you already know, for that information to be useful to you, you'll have to find your proportional allotment. To find your daily values, convert the per-serving grams or milligrams of each item on the label (which are based on a 2000-calorie diet) to the amount based on your daily calorie diet.

    **Example:** The food label on an energy bar lists the total fat as 2.5 grams, which is 4% of the daily allowance. Using that information, you can calculate the total daily allowance of fat grams:

    $$\frac{2.5}{4\%} = \frac{x}{100\%} \qquad x = 62.5 \text{ grams of fat per day for a 2000-calorie diet.}$$

*(continued)*

 *Real-Life Math: Algebra*

# 5.  How Much Can I Eat?

If you are allowed 3000 calories per day, then the daily allowance is:

$$\frac{62.5}{2000} = \frac{x}{3000}$$    $x = 94$ grams of fat per day

## Daily Values (Grams)

| | Total fat | Saturated fat | Cholesterol | Total carbohydrates |
|---|---|---|---|---|
| Daily allowance for 2000-calorie diet | 62.5 grams | | | |
| Your daily allowance | | | | |
| | **Dietary fiber** | **Sodium** | **Potassium** | **Protein** |
| Daily allowance for 2000-calorie diet | | | | |
| Your daily allowance | | | | |

3.    Choose a food label. Use the information in the daily value table to construct a personalized food label for yourself.

**Example:** If the energy bar label was customized for a 3000-calorie diet, for total fats the label would read

$$\frac{2.5}{94} = 0.0266,$$ or about 3% of your daily allowance

Custom nutritional label for (type of food): _____

## Daily Values (Percents)

| | Total fat | Saturated fat | Cholesterol | Total carbohydrates |
|---|---|---|---|---|
| Daily allowance for your diet | 62.5 grams | | | |
| | **Dietary fiber** | **Sodium** | **Potassium** | **Protein** |
| Daily allowance for your diet | | | | |

**13**  *Real-Life Math: Algebra*

# 6. How Steep Is It?

## Context

money

## Topic

ratios, proportions, and percents

## Overview

In this activity, students measure the access ramps at their school to determine their slope.

## Objectives

Students will be able to:

- set up ratios and determine slope

## Materials

- one copy of the Activity 6 handout for each student

- metersticks or yardsticks (two per group of students)

## Teaching Notes

- Students can work with a partner or in small groups for this activity.

- To measure the slope of a ramp using two measuring sticks, place one measuring stick along the side of the base of the ramp, with one end at the bottom edge of the slope. Place the second stick at a 90-degree angle to the first. Measure the distance on the

vertical measuring stick from the ground to the surface of the ramp at that point. This distance is the rise, or vertical distance. The horizontal distance will be the length of the measuring stick. You may need to demonstrate this procedure. See the diagram below.

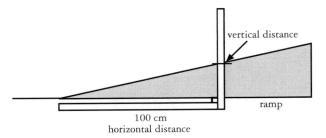

- If there are no access ramps at the school, students can conduct a similar investigation by finding the slope of stairs.

- If necessary, have students add rows to the table for additional ramps.

## Answers

Answers will vary depending on the slope of the access ramps at your school.

## Extension Activity

Have students investigate the Americans With Disabilities Act (ADA) and find other instances where mathematics plays an important role.

# 6.  How Steep Is It?

In July 1990, the U.S. government passed the Americans With Disabilities Act (ADA). An important part of the law requires that access ramps be built to meet certain specifications with regard to slope. By working through this investigation you will be able to determine if the access ramps at your school meet the specifications of the ADA.

## ADA Specifications for Access Ramps

The ADA specifies that the least slope possible should be used for any ramp. The maximum slope of a ramp in a new building should be 1:12. The maximum rise for any run should be 30 inches (760 millimeters). For ramps added to existing buildings with space limitations, a slope between 1:10 and 1:12 is allowed for a maximum rise of 6 inches; a slope between 1:8 and 1:10 is allowed for a maximum rise of 3 inches. A slope steeper than 1:8 is not allowed.

1.   Measure the access ramps at your school. Record your findings in the table below.

### Access Ramp Specifications

| Ramp location | Vertical measurement | Horizontal measurement | Ratio | Decimal equivalent | Percent equivalent |
|---|---|---|---|---|---|
| 1. | | | | | |
| 2. | | | | | |
| 3. | | | | | |
| 4. | | | | | |
| 5. | | | | | |

2.   Draft a memo to the principal stating the results of your investigation.

# 7. The Correct Dose

## Context

science/technology

## Topic

ratios, proportions, and percents

## Overview

In this activity, students use proportions to determine medicine dosing amounts.

## Objectives

Students will be able to:

- set up and solve problems using proportions

## Materials

- one copy of the Activity 7 handout for each student

## Teaching Notes

- Students can work individually or in pairs for this activity.

- Introduce the activity by asking students a question such as "How do you think doctors or nurses know how much medicine to give to a patient?"

- This activity presents a good opportunity to invite medical professionals from the community into the classroom to talk about how mathematics plays an important role in their jobs.

- You may want to make the school nurse off-limits for question 3.

## Answers

1. about 1500 mg

2–4. Answers will vary.

## Extension Activity

Have students investigate dosages for over-the-counter medicines.

# 7. The Correct Dose

Imagine you are a doctor or a nurse, and you have to prescribe the correct dosage of medicine for a young patient. The medicine's directions call for 55 milligrams per kilogram of body weight. How much medicine are you going to give the patient? Having paid attention in your algebra class, you know that you simply have to set up a proportion between the dosage amount and the patient's weight. You find out that the patient's weight is 37 pounds. Because you know that 1 kilogram is equal to 2.2 pounds, you divide 37 by 2.2 and find that the weight of the patient is 16.8 kilograms. Then you set up a proportion and solve for the correct dosage amount:

$$\frac{55mg}{1kg} = \frac{x}{16.8kg} \qquad x = 924 \text{ mg of medicine}$$

Now you're ready to administer the medicine. Answer the questions that follow regarding medicine dosing amounts.

The dosing amount for Augmentin, a common antibiotic, is 51.4 milligrams for each kilogram of body weight.

1. How many milligrams of Augmentin would you prescribe for a child who weighs 66 pounds?

   milligrams of Augmentin: _____

2. How many milligrams of Augmentin would a doctor prescribe for you?

   milligrams of Augmentin: _____

3. Contact some medical professionals and ask them how they determine the dosage amounts for patients. Describe the procedure below.

4. Based on the information you found out from the medical professionals, write a question that involves determining dosage amounts. Have another student solve your problem.

# 8. Can't Stop, We're Making Good Time

## Context

travel/transportation

## Topic

ratios, proportions, and percents

## Overview

In this activity, students determine how much time is saved by driving faster than the speed limit.

## Objectives

Students will be able to:

- set up and solve problems using proportions

- evaluate data

## Materials

- one copy of the Activity 8 handout for each student

- maps or road atlases (one per student)

## Teaching Notes

- Students should work individually on this lesson.

- Introduce the activity by modeling this driving situation with students. Let's say you're driving to visit someone who lives 100 miles away, and the speed limit is 65 miles per hour (mph). The

time it would take you to get there can be found using a ratio of distance to speed, or *d/s*. In this case, 100 mi/65 mph equals 1.54 hours, or 1 hour and 32 minutes. If the limit was 75 miles per hour, it would take you 1.33 hours, or 1 hour and 20 minutes. You would arrive at your destination 12 minutes sooner.

- For question 1, have students choose cities that are far apart. For question 2, students should choose cities that are relatively close together. This way they will see the relationship between speed and distance more clearly.

## Answers

1–2. Answers will vary depending on the distances between the two cities.

3. Students should mention that the greater the distance, the more time is saved.

## Extension Activity

Have students investigate the speed limits in different states for cars and for trucks.

# 8. Can't Stop, We're Making Good Time

From 1974 to 1995, the United States had a federal speed limit. In all 50 states, the maximum speed was 55 miles per hour. Since the law was repealed in 1995, most states have raised the speed limit for freeway driving. Since 1995, 31 states have raised the speed limit to 70 mph or higher on some part of their roadway system. Does a higher speed limit really get you from one place to another much faster? Let's find out.

1. Look at your map or road atlas and choose two cities that are far apart. Figure out the distance between them, and list the cities and the distance below. Then figure out how much time you would save driving from one city to the other at 75 mph instead of 55 mph.

   cities and distance between them: _____

   travel time difference: _____

2. Look at your map or road atlas again and select two cities that are relatively close together. Find the distance between the two cities. List the cities and the distance between them below. Then figure out how much time you would save driving from one city to the other by traveling at 65 mph instead of 55 mph.

   cities and distance between them: _____

   travel time difference: _____

3. What is the relationship among time saved, distance, and speed?

# 9. If You Build It, They Will Come

## Context

sports

## Topic

data and graphs

## Overview

In this activity, students act as a team of city council interns to create and submit a report that supports the construction of a new sports stadium for the city's baseball team.

## Objectives

Students will be able to:

- analyze and interpret data

- construct accurate scatter plots supported by narrative explanation

## Materials

- one copy of the Activity 9 handout for each student

- graph paper

## Teaching Notes

- Students can work in pairs or small groups for this activity.

- Students should be familiar with scatter plots prior to using this activity.

- Some students may not be sure where to begin. Lead them in the direction of using a scatter plot by asking questions such as "Which variable—

attendance or year built—is the dependent variable?"

- The report for this activity can be done using word processing software and a spreadsheet.

- The "Year" in the table represents the year in which the first game was played after new construction or major refurbishment of the stadium.

- This activity can provide a good opportunity to talk about the difference between correlation and cause and effect.

## Answers

In evaluating reports, look for accurate graphs and narratives that provide a full explanation of the relationship between attendance and the year the stadium was constructed or refurbished. Most students will note that there does appear to be a direct relationship between attendance and the year the stadium was built or refurbished. However, some students may recognize that the conclusion that the relationship is causal is questionable.

## Extension Activity

Ask students to investigate other potential explanations for attendance, including population base and team success.

## Data Resources

http://sports.espn.go.com/mlb/attendance

# 9. If You Build It, They Will Come

Imagine you and a group of your classmates are interns, doing a work-study assignment for your city council. The city council is trying to put together a convincing argument for building a new stadium for the professional baseball team in town. The council strongly supports a new stadium. They have looked at Major League Baseball (MLB) attendance data and are convinced that if a new stadium is built, attendance will increase. They have assigned your team the job of analyzing the attendance data for professional baseball teams and finding a relationship between attendance and the year a stadium was built or refurbished. The city council members will expect your report to include three things: graphs, a narrative section, and recommendations for more areas of study. The table below shows the data provided to your team.

### MLB Attendance for 2005 and Year the Stadium was Built or Refurbished

| American League | | | National League | | |
|---|---|---|---|---|---|
| Team | Attendance | Year stadium was built or refurbished | Team | Attendance | Year stadium was built or refurbished |
| Anaheim | 3,404,686 | 1993 | Arizona | 2,059,331 | 1998 |
| Baltimore | 2,624,804 | 1992 | Atlanta | 2,521,534 | 1997 |
| Boston | 2,813,354 | 1912 | Chicago | 3,100,262 | 1916 |
| Chicago | 2,342,834 | 1991 | Cincinnati | 1,943,157 | 2003 |
| Cleveland | 1,973,185 | 1994 | Colorado | 1,915,586 | 1995 |
| Detroit | 2,024,505 | 2000 | Florida | 1,823,388 | 1993 |
| Kansas City | 1,371,181 | 1973 | Houston | 2,762,472 | 2000 |
| Minnesota | 2,013,453 | 1982 | Los Angeles | 3,603,680 | 1962 |
| New York | 4,090,440 | 1976 | Milwaukee | 2,211,023 | 2001 |
| Oakland | 2,109,298 | 1968 | New York | 2,782,212 | 1964 |
| Seattle | 2,689,529 | 1999 | Philadelphia | 2,665,301 | 2004 |
| Texas | 2,486,925 | 1994 | Pittsburgh | 1,794,237 | 2001 |
| Toronto | 1,977,949 | 1989 | St. Louis | 3,491,837 | 2005 |
| | | | San Diego | 2,832,039 | 2004 |
| | | | San Francisco | 3,140,781 | 2000 |
| | | | Washington, DC | 2,692,123 | 2005 |

The first step in writing your report is to organize the data for analysis. Then your group will need to analyze the data and look for relationships that support the council's position. Then prepare a written report summarizing your group's findings.

# 10. Hot Wheels

## Context

money

## Topic

data and graphs

## Overview

In this activity, students analyze data regarding auto theft and insurance.

## Objectives

Students will be able to:

- analyze and interpret data

- construct accurate graphs

- calculate measures of central tendency and variation

## Materials

- one copy of the Activity 10 handout for each student

## Teaching Notes

- Students can work individually or in pairs on this activity.

- Graphing calculators are helpful for the type of statistical analysis in this activity.

- One possible way to introduce this activity is to pose an open question such as "What do you suppose is the average value of cars that are stolen most often?" Many students will assume that the higher a car's value, the more likely it is that the car will be stolen. This is not, however, the case.

- Many students will need a review of how to create a box-and-whisker plot. You may choose to make the computation of standard deviation optional.

## Answers

**Measures of Central Tendencies**

1.  mean: $4180
    median: $3175
    mode: no mode

2.  Answers will vary. In this type of data, median values are usually more indicative of the center because they are more resistant to extreme values.

3.  $Q_1$ = $1500; $Q_3$ = $5375

4.  Box-and-whisker plot should include:
    min = $175; $Q_1$ = $1500
    med = $3175; $Q_3$ = $5375
    max = $14,700

**Measures of Variability**

1.  The range of the data is $14,525.

2.  The standard deviation of the data is $3953.29.

*(continued)*

# 10. Hot Wheels

## Extension Activities

- Types of stolen cars and their values vary significantly by state. Have students research and analyze data for their own state.

- Ask students to predict what cars will be on the stolen car list next year, including make, model, year, and dollar value.

## Data Resources

https://www.nicb.org/cps/rde/xchg/SID-4031FE95-DEE6B11C/nicb/hs.xsl/211.htm

http://www.kbb.com

# 10. Hot Wheels

Every 20 seconds, a vehicle is stolen in the United States. What are the characteristics of the cars that are most frequently stolen? What might you do to reduce the chances that your car is stolen? The table below shows the ten cars stolen most often in 2004, according to the National Insurance Crime Bureau (NICB). Review the data, and then answer the questions that follow.

### Most Stolen Vehicles (2004) and Estimated Value

| Rank | Year | Make | Model | Value (in dollars) |
|------|------|------|-------|--------------------|
| 1 | 1995 | Honda | Civic | 5200 |
| 2 | 1989 | Toyota | Camry | 3150 |
| 3 | 1991 | Honda | Accord | 175 |
| 4 | 1994 | Dodge | Caravan | 1500 |
| 5 | 1994 | Chevy | 1500 (C/K) | 5375 |
| 6 | 1997 | Ford | F150 | 5600 |
| 7 | 2003 | Dodge | Ram Pickup | 14,700 |
| 8 | 1990 | Acura | Integra | 3200 |
| 9 | 1988 | Toyota | Pickup | 750 |
| 10 | 1991 | Nissan | Sentra | 2150 |

**Measures of Central Tendencies**

1.  Calculate the mean, median, and mode for the prices of the cars in the table.

    mean: _____

    median: _____

    mode: _____

*(continued)*

# 10. Hot Wheels

2.   Explain which of the numbers you found in question 1 best represents the data in the table.

3.   Find the first quartile (the median of the lower half of the data) and the third quartile (the median of the upper half of the data).

   $Q_1$ = _____

   $Q_3$ = _____

4.   Construct a box-and-whisker plot of the cars' values.

**Measures of Variability**

1.   What is the range of the data?

2.   What is the standard deviation for the price data?

# 11. Twister

## Context

science/technology

## Topic

data and graphs

## Overview

In this activity, students use tornado data to create scatter plots and find lines of best fit.

## Objectives

Students will be able to:

- analyze and interpret data

- create scatter plots

- find lines of best fit, correlation coefficients, and the equation of the line

## Materials

- one copy of the Activity 11 handout for each student

- graph paper

- graphing calculators

## Teaching Notes

- Students should work individually on this activity.

- Introduce the activity by eliciting from students what experiences they have had with tornadoes. Then pose a question such as "I wonder what the correlation is between the number of tornadoes in a state and the number of fatalities caused by tornadoes in that particular state?" Responses generally indicate the assumption that the higher the number of tornadoes, the higher the number of fatalities.

- This activity works well after students have studied lines of best fit and data correlation because the data do not fit especially well.

## Answers

1. Students should write a statement such as "The number of fatalities depends on the number of tornadoes."

2. Independent variable: number of tornadoes
   Dependent variable: fatalities
   Interval for $y$-axis: between 10 and 20
   Interval for $x$-axis: between 150 and 200

3. $r = 0.50338$
   Equation of the line of best fit:
   $y = 0.0593x + 79.92$

## Extension Activities

- Have students examine the data about adjusted damage on the table, then answer the questions using damage amounts instead of fatalities.

- Have students conduct additional research, such as fatalities per month and months with the most tornadoes.

## Data Resources

www.tornadoproject.com

# 11. Twister

Did you know that tornadoes occur in almost every state? However, some states experience a significantly higher number of tornadoes than others. For instance, in Oklahoma from 1950 to 1994, there were 2300 tornadoes. During the same period, California had only 214 tornadoes. Explore the tornado data below to learn more about this amazing weather phenomenon.

### Tornado Numbers and Deaths, 1950–1994

| Tornadoes | | | Deaths | | |
|---|---|---|---|---|---|
| rank | state | number | rank | state | number |
| 1 | TX | 5490 | 1 | TX | 475 |
| 2 | OK | 2300 | 7 | OK | 217 |
| 3 | KS | 2110 | 8 | KS | 199 |
| 4 | FL | 2009 | 19 | FL | 82 |
| 5 | NE | 1673 | 23 | NE | 1 |
| 6 | IA | 1374 | 22 | IA | 61 |
| 7 | MO | 1166 | 12 | MO | 155 |
| 8 | SD | 1139 | 28 | SD | 11 |
| 9 | IL | 1137 | 9 | IL | 182 |
| 10 | CO | 1113 | 38 | CO | 2 |
| 11 | LA | 1086 | 13 | LA | 134 |
| 12 | MS | 1039 | 2 | MS | 386 |

1. Look over the table and consider the relationship between the number of tornadoes and the number of tornado-related deaths in a state. Write a statement describing the relationship between the two sets of data.

*(continued)*

# 11. Twister

2.  Answer the questions below. Then, in the space below or on a sheet of graph paper, draw a scatter plot that shows the relationship between the number of tornadoes and the number of deaths in a state.

    independent variable: _____

    dependent variable: _____

    interval for *y*-axis: _____

    interval for *x*-axis: _____

3.  After you have constructed your scatter plot, use your graphing calculator to determine the line of best fit, the correlation coefficient, and the equation of the line.

    correlation coefficient, *r*, for the line of best fit: _____

    equation of your line of best fit: _____

# 12. Danger Zone

## Context

travel/transportation

## Topic

data and graphs

## Overview

In this activity, students analyze data on fatal car crashes.

## Objectives

Students will be able to:

- analyze and interpret data

- construct an accurate histogram

## Materials

- one copy of the Activity 12 handout for each student

## Teaching Notes

- Students should work individually on this activity.

- Introduce the activity by asking a question such as "Do you suppose there are certain times that it is more dangerous to be on the road than others?" Then ask students, "What are some reasons why certain times might be more dangerous than others?" If no students respond concerning alcohol, interject that idea into the conversation.

## Answers

1. midnight to 3 A.M., 78%
   3 A.M. to 6 A.M., 63%
   6 A.M. to 9 A.M., 22%
   9 A.M. to noon, 14%
   noon to 3 P.M., 18%
   3 P.M. to 6 P.M., 30%
   6 P.M. to 9 P.M., 52%
   9 P.M. to midnight, 66%

2. Histograms will vary but should show a relationship between late-night (after midnight) driving and alcohol-related crashes.

3. midnight to 3 A.M.

4. Because "likelihood" is based on a ratio of the number of accidents and the number of cars on the road, there is not enough data present to answer this question. However, most students will see that the largest number of fatal accidents occur between midnight and 3 A.M. and may answer that period. It might be good to discuss why that period has the highest number of crashes.

5. Answers will vary but should suggest avoiding driving from midnight until 3 A.M. (or 6 A.M.) when most alcohol-related accidents occur.

## Extension Activity

Have students research and evaluate other data involving car crashes.

## Data Resources

http://www.nhtsa.dot.gov

# 12. Danger Zone

Driving a car can be dangerous, but there are ways to increase your safety. One way is to avoid driving when it's most dangerous to be on the road. Complete the activity below to find out how to decrease your chances of becoming a traffic fatality.

### Total and Alcohol-Related Fatal Car Crashes by Time of Day

| Time of day | Number of fatal crashes | Number of alcohol-related fatal crashes | Percent of alcohol-related fatal crashes |
|---|---|---|---|
| midnight to 3 A.M. | 3962 | 3097 | |
| 3 A.M. to 6 A.M. | 2314 | 1457 | |
| 6 A.M. to 9 A.M. | 1982 | 442 | |
| 9 A.M. to noon | 1762 | 255 | |
| noon to 3 P.M. | 2286 | 401 | |
| 3 P.M. to 6 P.M. | 2994 | 891 | |
| 6 P.M. to 9 P.M. | 3642 | 1875 | |
| 9 P.M. to midnight | 3825 | 2531 | |

Source: National Highway Safety Administration, 2003 Annual Report

1. For each time period in the table, calculate the percentage of fatal crashes that are alcohol-related. List the percentages in the last column of the table.

2. On a separate sheet of paper or using a spreadsheet program, construct a histogram showing the relationship between time of day and percentage of fatal crashes that are alcohol-related.

3. During what time of day is a fatal accident most likely to involve alcohol?

4. During what time of day are you most likely to be involved in a fatal car accident?

5. What are some ways to reduce the likelihood of being involved in an alcohol-related accident?

**teacher's page**

# 13. Only a Matter of Time

## Context

sports

## Topic

systems of equations

## Overview

In this activity, students assume the role of a sportswriter who has been assigned to write an article comparing the performance of men and women in sporting events.

## Objectives

Students will be able to:

- analyze and interpret data

- derive linear equations from data

- graph and interpret linear equations

- use data and graphs to draw conclusions

## Materials

- one copy of the Activity 13 handout for each student

- graph paper

- graphing calculators

- reference material that contains historical sports information, such as almanacs and sports encyclopedias

## Teaching Notes

- Students can work individually or in pairs on this activity.

- Introduce the activity by asking a question such as "Do you suppose there are any athletic events in which men's and women's winning times are the same?" You may want to follow up with a question such as "Is it possible that in the future, women will surpass men in certain athletic events?"

- It's difficult to compare men's and women's sporting events because often all factors are not equal. It is best to consider timed sporting events in which the format and conditions of the event are identical.

- Some students are unsure of how to begin constructing a graph. Make sure those students are clear on how to select axes and appropriate intervals.

- Likewise, when they are using graphing calculators, many students have difficulty choosing appropriate settings for their graphs. Review this procedure prior to using the activity.

- Students should have some familiarity working with lines of best fit and doing linear regressions.

*(continued)*

**teacher's page**

# 13. Only a Matter of Time

## Answers

1. List "Year" on the $x$-axis and "Time" on the $y$-axis. The $x$-axis interval should be 4–10 years; the $y$-axis interval should be about 5 seconds.

2. $m = -0.161$; $b = 368.8$

3. line of best fit: $y = -0.161x + 368.8$

4. yes

5. $m = -0.2413$; $b = 535$

6. line of best fit: $y = -0.2413x + 535$

7. year: 2070; time: 35.57 seconds

8. This point represents when men's and women's times will be equal.

## Extension Activity

Have students explain why men's and women's times are converging in certain sporting events.

**32**

# 13. Only a Matter of Time

Imagine you have been hired as a sportswriter for a new sports magazine. Your new boss, the magazine's editor, has just reviewed the latest demographic report of its readership and is concerned about the magazine's shortage of female readers. This is a new magazine, and the editor wants to increase readership. He can't afford to let half the market slip away. So the editor assigns you the job of writing an article that highlights female athletes. After doing some initial research, you notice a trend in sporting events in which men and women compete against the clock. You have done your research and have collected a lot of data, and you are now ready to analyze the data to support your article.

The winning times and years for the men's and women's Olympic 100-meter freestyle are listed in the tables below. Use the information to answer the questions that follow.

### Men's 100-Meter Freestyle

| Year | Time (seconds) |
|------|------|
| 1920 | 61.4 |
| 1924 | 59.0 |
| 1928 | 58.6 |
| 1932 | 58.2 |
| 1936 | 57.6 |
| 1948 | 57.3 |
| 1952 | 57.4 |
| 1956 | 55.4 |
| 1960 | 55.2 |
| 1964 | 53.4 |
| 1968 | 52.2 |
| 1972 | 51.2 |
| 1976 | 50.0 |
| 1980 | 50.4 |
| 1984 | 49.8 |
| 1988 | 48.6 |
| 1992 | 49.0 |
| 1994 | 48.7 |
| 1996 | 48.7 |
| 2000 | 48.3 |
| 2004 | 48.17 |

### Women's 100-Meter Freestyle

| Year | Time (seconds) |
|------|------|
| 1920 | 73.6 |
| 1924 | 72.4 |
| 1928 | 71.0 |
| 1932 | 66.8 |
| 1936 | 65.9 |
| 1948 | 66.3 |
| 1952 | 66.8 |
| 1956 | 62.0 |
| 1960 | 61.2 |
| 1964 | 59.5 |
| 1968 | 60.0 |
| 1972 | 58.6 |
| 1976 | 55.7 |
| 1980 | 54.8 |
| 1984 | 55.9 |
| 1988 | 54.9 |
| 1992 | 54.6 |
| 1994 | 54.5 |
| 1996 | 54.5 |
| 2000 | 53.83 |
| 2004 | 53.84 |

Source: www.databaseolympics.com

*(continued)*

       *Real-Life Math: Algebra*

# 13. Only a Matter of Time

Answer the questions below and then construct a graph using the data from the table.

1. Explain which data set will go on the *x*-axis and which will go on the *y*-axis. Then select appropriate intervals for your graph.

   interval for *x*-axis: _____    interval for *y*-axis: _____

2. Using the data for men's times, plot the points on your graph, and determine if a linear relationship exists. If so, draw a line of best fit for the points.

   What is the slope (*m*) of the line of best fit? _____

   What is the *y*-intercept (*b*)? _____

3. Write an equation that represents the line of best fit.

Answer the questions below and follow the steps to plot the data from the women's 100-meter freestyle table on the same graph you used for the men's times.

4. Will the intervals you selected for the men's times work with the women's times?

5. Plot the points on your graph and determine if a linear relationship exists. If so, draw a line of best fit for the points.

   What is the slope (*m*) of the line of best fit? _____

   What is the *y*-intercept (*b*)? _____

6. Write an equation that represents the line of best fit.

## Point of Intersection

7. Extend the two lines on your graph until they intersect. At what year and time do the graphs intersect?

   year: _____    time: _____

8. What is the significance of the point of intersection on the graph?

## Write the Article

Research, collect, and analyze data for another sporting event that will support your position for the article. Write your article using both events as evidence. Display your data so that it is clear and easily understood.

# 14. Rising Tuition

## Context

money

## Topic

systems of equations

## Overview

In this activity, students examine public university tuition costs and how investments over time might meet those costs.

## Objectives

Students will be able to:

- analyze and interpret data

- derive linear equations from data

- graph and interpret linear equations

- use data and graphs to draw conclusions

## Materials

- one copy of the Activity 14 handout for each student

- graph paper

- graphing calculators

## Teaching Notes

- Students can work individually or in pairs on this activity.

- Many students are unaware of current college costs. Introduce the activity by eliciting from students how much they think college tuition costs are.

- College costs tend to rise faster than inflation, so assuming a 3% cost increase per year may not be accurate.

- For the section on investments, students will need to use the compounded interest formula in Activity 26.

- Many students are unsure of how to begin to construct a graph. Review graphing fundamentals with those students.

- When they are using graphing calculators, many students have difficulty choosing appropriate graph settings. Review this procedure prior to using the activity.

- Students should have some familiarity with working with lines of best fit and with doing linear regressions.

*(continued)*

# 14. Rising Tuition

## Answers

1. Dependent variable: tuition cost; independent variable: year. Sample sentence: The cost of tuition is dependent on the year.

2. Scales will vary. Years should be in increments of 1, but tuition cost may be in increments of $100, $200, or even $500.

3. Graphs will vary.

4. Possible equation:
   $y = 382.4x - 761,200$

5. Answers will vary. For example, if a student is 16 in 2007, then his or her child might attend college in 2037. Have students who are older than high-school age assume that they are 16 for the purposes of this activity.

6. Answers will vary, depending on answers to question 5.

## Extension Activity

Have students work a similar activity using private university tuition costs.

# 14. Rising Tuition

A lot of reports say college costs are skyrocketing out of control. This may be true for private colleges, but tuition costs for public institutions seem to rise in a steady pattern. The information in the table lists the college tuition costs for four-year public institutions of higher education since the 1999–2000 school year.

### College Tuition Costs, 1999–2000 to 2006–2007

| Year | Cost ($) |
|------|----------|
| 1999–2000 | 3362 |
| 2000–01 | 3487 |
| 2001–02 | 3725 |
| 2002–03 | 4115 |
| 2003–04 | 4694 |
| 2004–05 | 5126 |
| 2005–06 | 5491 |
| 2006–07 | 5836 |

Source: www.collegeboard.com

1. If you were to use the information in the table to construct a graph, which item would be the independent variable and which item would be the dependent variable? Write a sentence describing the relationship between the two variables.

   dependent variable: _____

   independent variable: _____

2. What interval will you use for the dependent and independent variables?

   dependent variable interval: _____

   independent variable interval: _____

*(continued)*

# 14.  Rising Tuition

3.   Construct a graph using the information from the table.




4.   Draw a line of best fit on your graph and write an equation for that line.

equation: _____


5.   If you have a child when you turn 28, in what year will he or she most likely first attend college?


6.   Use your graph to answer the following question: What will the cost of tuition at a four-year public institution of higher education be when your child first enters college?

tuition cost per year: _____

four-year cost: _____

# 15. The Next Dell

## Context

science/technology

## Topic

systems of equations

## Overview

In this activity, students research costs of computer parts and compare expenses to income for a computer-business building.

## Objectives

Students will be able to:

- analyze and interpret data

- derive linear equations from data

- graph and interpret linear equations

- use data and graphs to draw conclusions

## Materials

- one copy of the Activity 15 handout for each student

- graph paper

- graphing calculators

- publications or online sources that have computer prices

## Teaching Notes

- Students can work individually, in pairs, or in small groups for this activity.

- Students don't necessarily have to know what each individual computer component is to complete the activity. However, this activity provides a good opportunity to work with technology instructors and talk about computer components and assembly.

- Some students will have difficulty deciding on pricing amounts. Have them consider the competition's pricing structure and the markup on everyday items they purchase.

- As computer technology advances, it may become necessary to update component specifications.

- Students should have some familiarity with working with lines of best fit and with doing linear regressions.

## Selected Answers

Computer component costs vary. Expect about $1400 per computer for parts.

## Extension Activities

- Have students add $250 in advertising to their start-up costs, then write a new expense equation, predict how the equation will affect the point of intersection, and graph the new equation to verify their predictions.

- Have students research how other businesses got their start.

# 15. The Next Dell

Do you think it is possible to start a multi-billion-dollar company in your college dorm room? Michael Dell, founder of Dell Computers, started his company over 20 years ago in his college dorm room. Since then, Dell has become one of the largest manufacturers of computers in the world, with over 69,700 employees. Every day, new businesses start up in people's garages, living rooms, and kitchens. With luck and diligence, you could be next.

Imagine you and a friend decide to start a company that builds computers. After a while, word gets out about your great computers, and you start receiving orders. A small company asks you to make a bid for supplying them with 10 computers with the following specifications:

- Intel 3.6 GHz Pentium 4 Processor
- 800 MHz FSB w/1.0 GB SDRam
- 19-inch flat-panel monitor
- 128 MB ATI Radeon X600SE video card
- keyboard
- tower case
- 80 GB SATA 3.0 $^{Gb}/_s$

- 80 GB SATA 3.0 $^{Gb}/_s$
- 8 MB databurst cache
- 16X DVD +/- RW
- AS501 speakers
- mouse

1. Use computer magazines, the newspaper, or online resources to find the cost of parts to build a computer such as the one listed above.

   total cost per computer: _____

2. Fill in the expense column for each number of computers in the table. Assume that start-up costs for your company will be $2000.

| Number of computers | 1 | 2 | 3 | 4 | 5 | 10 | 15 | 30 | 45 | 75 |
|---------------------|---|---|---|---|---|----|----|----|----|----|
| Expense | | | | | | | | | | |
| Income | | | | | | | | | | |

*(continued)*

# 15. The Next Dell

3.  Write an equation that represents the expense of building *n* computers.

4.  Consider how much profit you want to make from each computer, then fill in the income section of the table.

5.  Write an equation that represents income for *n* computers sold.

6.  How many computers do you have to sell to make a profit?

7.  If you were to graph the two equations, at what point would the two lines intersect?

8.  Graph the two equations. Did the lines intersect where you predicted?

9.  What does the point of intersection represent on your graph?

*Real-Life Math: Algebra*

# 16. Surf's Up!

## Context

travel/transportation

## Topic

systems of equations

## Overview

In this activity, students listen in on a conversation between a pair of surfboard entrepreneurs and then help them plan their business.

## Objectives

Students will be able to:

- analyze and interpret data
- derive linear equations from data
- graph and interpret linear equations
- use data and graphs to draw conclusions

## Materials

- one copy of the Activity 16 handout for each student
- graph paper
- graphing calculators

## Teaching Notes

- Students can work individually or in pairs on this activity.

- Many students are unsure of how to begin to construct a graph. Review graphing fundamentals with those students.

- Likewise, when they are using graphing calculators, many students have difficulty choosing appropriate graph settings. Review this procedure prior to using the activity.

- Students should have some familiarity with working with lines of best fit and with doing linear regressions.

## Answers

1.  1 board: $150        10 boards: $1500
    2 boards: $300       15 boards: $2250
    3 boards: $450       20 boards: $3000
    4 boards: $600       25 boards: $3750
    5 boards: $750

2.  Income will vary depending on price.

3.  Expense equation: $y = 150n + 1000$
    Income equations will vary depending on price but will likely be
    $x = (600 - 150) n - 1000$.

4.  3 surfboards

## Extension Activity

Have students explore start-up costs, expenses, and income for other businesses.

# 16. Surf's Up!

The following conversation took place somewhere on a beach in southern California:

> Dustin: "You know, like, I saw you out there shredding. You have a, like, killer board, dude. Where did ya get it?"

> Beau: "I made the board myself, dude, and others, too. My dad has a shop with all the tools and stuff."

> Dustin: "No way!"

> Beau: "For sure. Like, did you see the way I dropped in on that gnarly tube? I was totally stoked."

> Dustin: "Ya, like, totally killer. Ya know, you should, like, sell some of those radical boards so, like, you could, you know, like, make some cash."

> Beau : "No way! That would be totally radical. Let's do it."

> Dustin: "For sure."

Help Beau and Dustin set up their surfboard business by working through the activity below.

1. Beau and Dustin figure that it costs about $150 in materials to build a surfboard. Fill in the cost of materials section of the table below.

| Number of boards | 1 | 2 | 3 | 4 | 5 | 10 | 15 | 20 | 25 |
|---|---|---|---|---|---|---|---|---|---|
| Cost of materials | | | | | | | | | |
| Income | | | | | | | | | |

2. Beau and Dustin assume that to be competitive in the surfboard market, they will have to keep the surfboard price below $600. They also figure they will have to spend about $1000 on start-up costs such as advertising and materials. Decide on a price for the boards, then fill in the income section of the table.

3. Write equations to represent expenses and income.

   expenses:

   income:

4. Graph the equations. How many surfboards will Beau and Dustin have to sell to break even?

# 17. Fitness Evaluation

## Context

sports

## Topic

systems of equations

## Overview

In this activity, students must use their algebra skills to make fitness charts for new members at the YMCA.

## Objectives

Students will be able to:

- analyze and interpret data
- derive linear equations from data
- graph and interpret linear equations
- use data and graphs to draw conclusions

## Materials

- one copy of the Activity 17 handout for each student
- graph paper
- graphing calculators

## Teaching Notes

- Students can work in small groups on this activity.
- Introduce the activity by asking a question such as "Does anyone know

how to measure the intensity level you are exercising at?"

- Model for the class how to take your pulse.

- Many students are unsure of how to begin to construct a graph. Review graphing fundamentals with those students.

- Likewise, when they are using graphing calculators, many students have difficulty choosing appropriate settings for their graphs. Review this procedure prior to using the activity.

- Students should have some familiarity with working with lines of best fit and with doing linear regressions.

## Answers

1–3. Answers will vary depending upon students' ages and resting pulse rates.

4. Students may recognize that resting pulse rate changes as level of fitness changes.

5. Answers will vary but may discuss age-related health conditions.

## Extension Activity

Students can monitor their resting pulse rate over time and see how it affects target heart rate calculation.

# 17. Fitness Evaluation

Imagine you've just been hired to work at the local YMCA as a fitness evaluator. As part of your job, you will help new members set up target heart rate charts. Heart rate is typically a good measure of intensity during aerobic exercise. Because you start work in a couple days, you want to practice making heart rate charts for yourself and some of your friends. Follow the steps below to learn how to make target heart rate charts.

**Resting Pulse**

The first bit of information you need to gather is resting pulse rates for you and your friends. Before you measure your pulse, make sure you have been sitting quietly for a short while. On a separate sheet of paper, record the resting pulse rates of you and your friends.

**Target Heart Rate**

The Karvonen formula, shown below, is used to determine target heart rates based on age, resting pulse rate, and exercise fitness level. Use the formula to calculate target heart rates for three different fitness levels: beginner, average, and high.

target heart rate = (220 − age − resting pulse rate) × (fitness level) + (resting pulse rate)

average: 0.7     beginner: 0.6     high: 0.8

1.  Based on your current age, calculate your target heart rate for each fitness level.

    beginner: _____    average: _____    high: _____

2.  Make a graph showing a comparison between target heart rate and age. Plot the data for your current age.

3.  As you age, your target heart rate will change. Calculate how your target heart rate might change over the next 30 years. Plot those points on your graph.

4.  Write an equation that could be used to determine your target heart rate for any age and for each level of fitness.

    beginner: _____

    average: _____

    high: _____

5.  As you age, what other factors might you take into consideration regarding your target heart rate?

**teacher's page**

# 18. Air Time

## Context

money

## Topic

systems of equations

## Overview

In this activity, students assume the role of a sales rep who is tasked with recommending a new cell phone plan to the supervisor.

## Objectives

Students will be able to:

- analyze and interpret data
- derive linear equations from data
- graph and interpret linear equations
- use data and graphs to draw conclusions

## Materials

- one copy of the Activity 18 handout for each student
- graph paper
- graphing calculators

## Teaching Notes

- This activity works best for individual students.
- Many students are unsure of how to begin to construct a graph. Review graphing fundamentals with those students.

- Likewise, when they are using graphing calculators, many students have difficulty choosing appropriate settings for their graphs. Review this procedure prior to using the activity.

- Students should have some familiarity with working with lines of best fit and with doing linear regressions.

## Answers

1.  Answers will vary, but 880, 1100, and 1320 are about the right values.

2.  plan 1: $y = .40(n \times 900) + 59.99$

    plan 2: $y = .10(n \times 1000) + 59.99$

    plan 3: $y = .10(n \times 1400) + 79.99$

3.  Answers will vary.

4.  Students should be able to find the values of $n$ for which the plan costs are equal.

5.  Answers will vary.

6.  Answers will vary, but encourage thoughtful, complete, and careful support for students' choices.

## Extension Activity

Have students make a formal presentation using software such as Microsoft PowerPoint.

## Data Resources

http://myrateplan.letstalk.com

# 18. Air Time

Imagine you are a sales rep for a soft drink company. Your district manager has asked you, one of the twelve sales reps she supervises, to submit a report recommending a replacement plan for your current cell phone service. You calculate that each sales rep uses his or her cell phone, on average, between 40 and 60 minutes each weekday. Use the information in the table to select which of the three plans would be most cost-efficient for your company. Then write a report detailing your selection and reasoning.

### Cell Phone Calling Plans

| Plan | Monthly contract cost | Monthly minutes included in plan | Additional airtime charges (per minute) |
|------|-----------------------|----------------------------------|------------------------------------------|
| Plan 1 | $59.99 | 900 | $0.40 |
| Plan 2 | $59.99 | 1000 | $0.10 |
| Plan 3 | $79.99 | 1400 | $0.10 |

1.  First you will probably want to figure out how many minutes per month each sales rep will use a phone. Because you are estimating their usage, you will want to evaluate a range of times. Decide on at least three times—low, medium, and high.

    low: _____     medium: _____     high: _____

2.  Next, write an equation to represent each of the three plans in the table.

    Plan 1: _____

    Plan 2: _____

    Plan 3: _____

*(continued)*

# 18. Air Time

3. Calculate the cost of each plan based on the different monthly usage amounts.

   Plan 1

   low usage: _____ medium usage: _____ high usage: _____

   Plan 2

   low usage: _____ medium usage: _____ high usage: _____

   Plan 3

   low usage: _____ medium usage: _____ high usage: _____

4. Construct a graph that shows where the rates for the different phone plans overlap.

5. Assess the pros and cons of the different plans and select the plan that you will recommend to your district manager.

6. Write a recommendation that includes a detailed analysis of the advantages of the plan you have selected.

**48**

**teacher's page**

# 19. Alternative Fuels

## Context

science/technology

## Topic

systems of equations

## Overview

In this activity, students investigate the costs associated with operating alternative fuel vehicles.

## Objectives

Students will be able to:

- graph and interpret linear equations

- use data and graphs to draw conclusions

## Materials

- one copy of the Activity 19 handout for each student

- graph paper

- graphing calculators

## Teaching Notes

- Students can work individually or in pairs on this activity.

- To answer question 2, students will have to estimate how many gallons of gas they might use in a year.

## Answers

1.  natural gas: $186n$

    propane: $202n$

    ethanol: $243n$

    gasoline: $226n$

2–3.  Answers will vary based on level of usage.

4.  Answers will vary but a $2000 investment will either offset savings or add to increase in first year(s).

5.  Answers will vary.

6.  pros: better for the environment, long-term savings
    cons: intial cost

## Extension Activities

- Have students research other types of alternative fuel vehicles and their costs.

- Research how alternative fuel vehicles are used locally.

# 19. Alternative Fuels

Engineers and scientists are working to make electric cars practical for everyday use. But did you know that there are other types of alternative fuel vehicles that use natural gas and propane already operating in the United States? In fact, it is estimated that there are 650,000 alternative fuel vehicles on the road today. Alternative fuels cause less pollution than gasoline or diesel fuels. So if the technology exists to build alternative fuel vehicles, and if they pollute less than gasoline or diesel cars, why doesn't everyone drive one? Maybe the issue is the cost of operating these vehicles. Work through the activity and decide if cost is preventing the widespread use of alternative fuel vehicles.

To compare fuel prices, alternative fuels are sold in gasoline-gallon equivalents (gges), which will get you as far down the road as a gallon of gasoline would. This makes prices at the station directly comparable. At a public fueling site in Dubuque, Iowa, natural gas sells for $1.86 per gge, propane sells for $2.02 per gge, and ethanol (E85) sells for $2.43 per gge. Local gasoline prices are $2.26 per gallon for 87-octane, regular unleaded gas.

Source: www.eere.energy.gov

1. Write an equation that represents the cost per number of gallons (or gges) for each type of fuel.

   natural gas: _____

   propane: _____

   ethanol: _____

   gasoline: _____

2. On a separate sheet of paper, construct a table that shows a comparison between the costs of the different fuels over a year's time for your level of usage.

3. What could the difference in fuel costs be for your usage during the course of a year?

4. If it costs $2000 to convert a gasoline vehicle to an alternative fuel vehicle, how would that affect the yearly fuel costs?

5. How does the cost of operating an alternative fuel vehicle compare to that of operating a gasoline vehicle?

6. What are some of the pros and cons of alternative fuel vehicles?

**teacher's page**

# 20. Buying versus Leasing

## Context

travel/transportation

## Topic

systems of equations

## Overview

In this activity, students evaluate the pros and cons of leasing and buying a new vehicle.

## Objectives

Student will be able to:

- analyze and interpret data
- derive linear equations from data
- graph and interpret linear equations

## Materials

- one copy of the Activity 20 handout for each student
- graph paper
- graphing calculators
- classified ads sections from newspapers or online resources

## Teaching Notes

- Students can work individually or in pairs on this activity.
- Introduce the activity by asking a general question such as "Does anyone know what some of the differences are between leasing and buying a new car?"
- Monthly payments represent most of the cost of leasing or buying a new car. However, there are other expenses, such as down payments, mileage fees, and repairs.
- Many students are unsure of how to begin to construct a graph. Review graphing fundamentals with those students.
- Likewise, when they are using graphing calculators, many students have difficulty choosing appropriate settings for their graphs. Review this procedure prior to using the activity.
- Students should have some familiarity with working with lines of best fit and with doing linear regressions.

## Answers

Answers will vary depending on car selected.

## Extension Activities

- Have students discuss the advantages and disadvantages of buying and leasing a car.
- Have students investigate depreciation and how it affects the value of a car over time.

# 20. Buying versus Leasing

Many people choose to lease a new car rather than buy one, enticed by the low monthly payments and low down payments featured in lease advertising. So if you pay lower monthly payments by leasing rather than buying a car, then leasing is a better deal—right? Complete the activity below to help you decide which is a better deal—leasing or buying.

1.  Look at the new car advertisements in the classified section of your newspaper or on the Internet. You'll notice that some of them list a monthly payment amount and the car's selling price. The monthly payment amount is generally a per-month lease payment, and the price is the cash amount. Find a car ad that lists cash prices and lease payment amounts.

    car: _____     lease payment: _____     cash price: _____

2.  Assuming you will finance the entire cost of the vehicle, calculate the monthly payment for the car using the formula below, where $m$ = the monthly payment, $A$ = the amount of the loan, $r$ = the annual interest rate (expressed as a decimal), and $n$ = the number of months of the loan. For this loan, assume an interest rate of 8% and a loan of 60 months (5 years).

    $$m = \frac{A(\frac{r}{12})(1 + \frac{r}{12})^n}{(1 + \frac{r}{12})^n - 1}$$

    monthly loan payment: _____

3.  Build a table that shows the cumulative cost for leasing and buying the car. Assume that, when the initial lease is up, you will lease another car for a similar payment.

| Number of months | 1 | 6 | 12 | 18 | 24 | 30 | 36 | 48 | 60 | 72 |
|---|---|---|---|---|---|---|---|---|---|---|
| Leasing | | | | | | | | | | |
| Buying | | | | | | | | | | |

4.  Make a graph that shows the cumulative payments over the next 7 years.

5.  At the time the lease expires, what is the sum of monthly payments for the lease and the loan?

    lease: _____          loan: _____

6.  At the end of 6 years, what is the sum of monthly payments for the lease and the loan?

    lease: _____          loan: _____

**teacher's page**

# 21. What's My Risk?

## Context

sports

## Topic

quadratics

## Overview

In this activity, students measure their body mass index (BMI) to determine their level of risk for certain diseases.

## Objectives

Students will be able to:

- apply and use BMI formulas

- construct accurate graphs

- analyze and interpret data

## Materials

- one copy of the Activity 21 handout for each student

- graph paper

- graphing calculators

## Teaching Notes

- Students should work in pairs or small groups for this activity.

- Prior to the activity, students will need to determine their weight and height.

- Many students are unsure of how to begin to construct a graph. Review graphing fundamentals with those students.

- Likewise, when they are using graphing calculators, many students have difficulty choosing appropriate settings for their graphs. Review this procedure prior to using the activity.

- Students should have some familiarity with working with lines of best fit and with doing linear regressions.

- Students shouldn't be alarmed if their BMI indicates that they are in a high-risk category. Simply advise them to consult a doctor or other medical professional.

- Some students may be sensitive about their weight. If so, you could assign a height and weight to each student.

## Answers

1–6. Answers will vary depending on students' heights and weights.

7. Students should point out that height is essentially a constant, not actually a squared term.

## Extension Activity

Students can research other instances in which mathematical formulas are used for fitness measurements.

# 21. What's My Risk?

Body mass index (BMI) is a measure of the ratio between your weight and your height squared. If your BMI is high, you may have an increased risk of developing certain diseases, such as adult-onset diabetes, cardiovascular disease, and hypertension. To find out your level of risk, and how changing your weight affects your risk level, follow the steps below.

1.  To find your BMI, first measure your height and weight. With your partner or in your group, measure each other's height in inches and record the result below. Likewise, weigh yourself in pounds and record the result below.

    height (inches): _____          weight (pounds): _____

2.  The formula used to calculate BMI requires metric units. Convert your height and weight to metric units using the conversion factors listed.

    inches × 0.0254 = meters          pounds × 0.4536 = kilograms

    height (meters): _____          weight (kilograms): _____

3.  Calculate your BMI using the formula below:

    $$BMI = \frac{weight\,(kg)}{height^2\,(m^2)}$$          BMI = _____

| BMI | Health risk |
|---|---|
| <25 | minimal |
| 25–27 | low |
| 27–30 | moderate |
| 30–35 | high |
| 35–40 | very high |
| 40+ | extremely high |

4.  On a separate sheet of paper, construct a graph that shows the relationship between BMI and weight for someone your height.

5.  Write an equation that represents the data in your graph.

6.  Explain the relationship between BMI and weight. Then explain the relationship between BMI and height.

7.  Explain why the data don't fit a quadratic curve even though one of the terms in your equation is squared.

# 22. Pizza by the Inch

## Context

money

## Topic

quadratics

## Overview

In this activity, students work with a partner to design a menu and pricing structure for a new pizza restaurant.

## Objectives

Students will be able to:

- apply and use area formulas

- graph quadratic formulas

## Materials

- one copy of the Activity 22 handout for each student

- graph paper

- graphing calculators

## Teaching Notes

- Students can work individually or in pairs on this activity.

- Introduce the activity by asking a general question such as "How much does a pepperoni pizza cost?" From there, elicit from students how pizzas are priced.

- You may want to collect flyers or take-out menus from pizza restaurants for the activity.

- For question 2, you may need to prompt students to draw a graph showing the relationship between side or diameter length and area.

- Students may need help getting started on pricing pizzas. This presents a good opportunity for students to set up simple equations and solve for the price based on what they want the final price to be. Remind students that the square and round pizzas will be priced the same.

- Many students are unsure of how to begin to construct a graph. Review graphing fundamentals with those students.

- Likewise, when they are using graphing calculators, many students have difficulty choosing appropriate settings for their graphs. Review this procedure prior to using the activity.

## Answers

1. 

| Square pizza | Round pizza |
|---|---|
| 5 = 25 | 6 = 9.42 |
| 6 = 36 | 7 = 10.99 |
| 7 = 49 | 8 = 12.56 |
| 8 = 64 | 9 = 14.13 |
| 9 = 81 | 10 = 15.70 |
| 10 = 100 | 11 = 17.27 |
| 11 = 121 | 12 = 18.84 |
| 12 = 144 | 13 = 20.41 |
| 13 = 169 | 14 = 21.98 |

*(continued)*

# 22. Pizza by the Inch

2. Students should draw a graph of the area function, or they may elect to build a more detailed table.

3. Prices will vary; however, the price per square inch of cheese pizza will most likely be between 9 and 14 cents.

4. Prices will vary.

## Extension Activity

In what other unique ways could students design a restaurant and use formulas for pricing or portion size?

**56**

# 22. Pizza by the Inch

Imagine you and a friend are starting a new pizza restaurant. The two of you have come up with a marketing idea that you think will help you stand out from the pack. You will sell two different shapes of pizza, square and round, but instead of offering set prices and sizes, you will allow customers to order pizza based on side length or diameter. The pizzas will be priced by their area. In other words, you will charge per square inch of pizza. However, before you can open the restaurant, you have to create a menu and determine prices. Follow the steps below to create the menu and set the prices for your new pizza restaurant.

**Square Pizzas**

1.  To make the square pizzas, you've found pans that can be adjusted to fit side lengths between 5 and 13 inches to the nearest quarter inch. You know that the area of a square is equal to the length of its side squared, so you decide to construct a table that shows the area for each side length. Fill in the table below. Leave the price section blank for now.

| Side length (inches) | 5 | 6 | 7 | 8 | 9 | 10 | 11 | 12 | 13 |
|---|---|---|---|---|---|---|---|---|---|
| Area (square inches) | | | | | | | | | |
| Price (cheese) | | | | | | | | | |

2.  A customer may order a pizza with a 7 3/4-inch side. You'll need an easy way for your employees to figure the area quickly. How might you provide this information in a format that is easy and quick to use?

3.  Next you will have to figure out how much to charge per square inch. You will also want to price the pizzas differently, depending on the number or types of toppings. For example, cheese, pepperoni, or both cheese and pepperoni would cost different amounts per square inch. As you decide on your per-square-inch prices, consider how much you might pay for a comparably sized pizza at another restaurant. When you are finished filling in the price-per-square-inch table on the next page, go back to the first table and complete the per-pizza price section.

*(continued)*

# 22. Pizza by the Inch

| Toppings | | | | | |
|---|---|---|---|---|---|
| Price per square inch | | | | | |

## Round Pizzas

1.  To make the round pizzas, you've found pans that can be adjusted to fit pizzas with diameters between 6 and 14 inches to the nearest quarter inch. You know that the area of a circle is equal to the radius squared times *pi* ($\pi$), so you decide to construct a table that shows the area for each diameter. Fill in the table below; leave the price section blank for now.

| Diameter (inches) | 6 | 7 | 8 | 9 | 10 | 11 | 12 | 13 | 14 |
|---|---|---|---|---|---|---|---|---|---|
| Area (square inches) | | | | | | | | | |
| Price (cheese) | | | | | | | | | |

2.  A customer may order a pizza with a $10\frac{1}{2}$-inch diameter. You'll need an easy way for your employees to figure the area quickly. How might you provide this information in a format that is easy and quick to use?

3.  Price the round pizzas using the same pricing structure you decided on for the square pizzas. Now fill in the price section of the table.

4.  Reevaluate the prices you chose for your pizzas and decide if you need to make any adjustments to your prices so that you're competitive in the pizza market.

## Menu

Create a menu that clearly explains your ordering and pricing procedures. Be sure that your menu is clear and easy for your customers to understand. You may want to include visual aids such as tables or graphs as part of your menu.

       *Real-Life Math: Algebra*

**teacher's page**

# 23. How Cold Is It?

## Context

science/technology

## Topic

quadratics

## Overview

In this activity, students derive a formula for calculating wind chill.

## Objectives

Students will be able to:

- derive quadratic equations from data
- graph and interpret quadratic equations
- use data and graphs to draw conclusions

## Materials

- one copy of the Activity 23 handout for each student
- graph paper
- graphing calculators
- outdoor thermometer

## Teaching Notes

- Students can work individually or in pairs on this activity.
- This activity works best during the cooler months.
- You may want to have students practice estimating wind speed using the Beaufort scale several times prior to using the activity.
- When students plot the data, make

sure they understand that all six temperatures in the table are plotted as separate curves. Likewise, students will need to derive an equation for each curve.

- Some students may have difficulty combining the equations into one general equation. This can be a good opportunity to discuss estimating and degree of accuracy.
- Many students are unsure of how to begin to construct a graph. Review graphing fundamentals with those students.
- Likewise, when they are using graphing calculators, many students have difficulty choosing appropriate settings for their graphs. Review this procedure prior to using the activity.
- Students should have some familiarity with working with curves of best fit and with doing quadratic regressions.

## Answers

1. Graphs will vary depending on scales used.
2. Sample equations:
   $20°: y = 0.024x^2 \times 2.074x + 21.89$
   $30°: y = 0.026x^2 \times 2.091x + 35.45$
3. Sample general equation:
   $$\text{wind chill} = \frac{windspeed^2}{40} - 2(windspeed) + \text{air temperature}$$
4. Compare student answers to temperature amounts in table: $-5°, 4°$

5–7. Answers will vary.

# 23. How Cold Is It?

Do you have a thermometer outside that you rely on to let you know how cold it is? If so, you are only getting half the story. A better measure of how cold it actually feels outside is wind chill, which combines the effects of the temperature and the wind. But to figure out wind chill, you must know how fast the wind is blowing and have a wind chill chart handy, right? Not anymore. With a little help from algebra and an old British admiral named Beaufort, by the end of this activity you will create an easy-to-use wind chill formula and learn how to estimate wind speed so you can calculate wind chill anytime with only a thermometer.

## Wind Chill Formula

Listed below is a partial chart of the wind chill index for temperatures from 10° to 35°F and for wind speeds from 0 to 35 mph.

### Wind Chill

| Wind speed (mph) | Wind chill (degrees Fahrenheit) | | | | | |
|---|---|---|---|---|---|---|
| 0 | 35 | 30 | 25 | 20 | 15 | 10 |
| 5 | 32 | 27 | 22 | 16 | 11 | 6 |
| 10 | 22 | 16 | 10 | 3 | −3 | −9 |
| 15 | 16 | 9 | 2 | −5 | −12 | −19 |
| 20 | 11 | 4 | −3 | −11 | −18 | −25 |
| 25 | 8 | −1 | −7 | −15 | −22 | −30 |
| 30 | 6 | −3 | −11 | −18 | −26 | −33 |
| 35 | 4 | −5 | −13 | −20 | −28 | −36 |

1.  On a separate sheet of paper, plot a curve showing the wind chill for each temperature given in the chart. List the temperature on the *y*-axis and wind speed on the *x*-axis. You will have to plot a different curve for each temperature, because wind chill for each temperature is represented by a different equation. Make sure to label each curve on your graph.

2.  Write an equation to represent each curve on your graph. List the equations below.

3.  Study the equations you wrote and combine them into one general equation that could be used to calculate wind chill. Make the equation as simple and easy to use as possible. You may want to use words to represent variables. Write the general equation below.

*(continued)*

# 23.  How Cold Is It?

4.  Test the accuracy of your equation by solving two problems. Calculate the wind chill for each situation below.

   a.  temperature 20°F, wind speed 15 mph

   b.  temperature 30°F, wind speed 20 mph

**Estimating Wind Speed**

The Beaufort scale is one of the most common methods used to estimate wind speed. Look over the scale, then practice estimating wind speed over the next couple days. Check your accuracy using a weather station at your school, or find the current weather conditions on television, the radio, or the Internet.

### Beaufort Wind Scale

| Wind speed | Description | Wind speed | Description |
|---|---|---|---|
| calm | tree leaves don't move, smoke rises vertically | 13–18 mph | small branches move, flags flap, dust, leaves and loose paper rise up |
| 1–3 mph | tree leaves don't move, smoke drifts slowly, weathervanes don't move | 19–24 mph | small trees sway, flags flap and ripple |
| 4–7 mph | tree leaves rustle, flags wave slightly, wind felt on face, weathervanes begin to move | 25–31 mph | large branches sway, flags beat and pop, whistling heard in wires |
| 8–12 mph | leaves and twigs in constant motion, small flags extended | 32–38 mph | whole trees sway, resistance felt when walking against wind |

5.  Now that you have created a user-friendly wind chill formula and have become an expert at estimating wind speed, you are ready to try out your new skills. Note the current temperature, estimate the current wind speed, and use your formula to figure out the wind chill. Try this at different times during the day and on days where conditions differ.

6.  Assess the accuracy of your formula by comparing your results with the actual wind chill.

7.  Explain how you could improve the accuracy of your wind chill formula, while still maintaining its ease of use.

Quadratics

# 24. Miles per Gallon

## Context

travel/transportation

## Topic

quadratics

## Overview

In this activity, students assume the role of a public relations specialist for an automobile manufacturer and analyze data to write a speech.

## Objectives

Students will be able to:

- graph and interpret quadratic equations

- derive quadratic equations from data

- use data and graphs to draw conclusions

## Materials

- one copy of the Activity 24 handout for each student

- graph paper

- graphing calculators

## Teaching Notes

- Students should do the graphing and regression individually. However, you may choose to allow them to work together to write the speech.

- Introduce the activity by asking a general question such as, "Do you think that cars have become more or less fuel efficient over the past 30 years?"

- Many students are unsure of how to begin to construct a graph. Review graphing fundamentals with those students.

- Likewise, when they are using graphing calculators, many students have difficulty choosing appropriate settings for their graphs. Review this procedure prior to using the activity.

- Students should have some familiarity with working with curves of best fit and with doing quadratic regressions.

## Answers

2. A good quadratic regression of this data yields the equation
$y = .0044x^2 \times 17.21x + 16,865$

3. 2010: 25.85

   2015: 28.24

   2020: 30.85

   2030: 36.73

4. Speeches will vary.

## Extension Activity

Students can investigate other advances in automobile technology that can be measured using algebra.

# 24.  Miles per Gallon

Imagine you work as a public relations specialist for a major domestic automobile manufacturer. The public relations supervisor has assigned you the responsibility of preparing a 5-minute speech for one of the division directors of the company. The director will be delivering the speech at an upcoming auto show and wants to highlight the company's long-term commitment to designing and building more fuel-efficient vehicles. You have gathered some historical data concerning fuel efficiency and are ready to analyze the data in support of the speech.

1.  Listed in the table below are the average fuel efficiency data (in miles per gallon) for U.S. passenger cars from 1950 to 2004. Make a graph using the information in the chart.

| Year | mpg |
|------|-----|
| 1950 | 14.8 |
| 1960 | 13.9 |
| 1970 | 13.4 |
| 1980 | 16.0 |
| 1990 | 20.2 |
| 2000 | 21.9 |
| 2004 | 22.4 |

Source: http://www.bts.gov/publications/national_transportation_statistics/

2.  Find the quadratic curve of best fit for this data and write the equation below.



3.  Estimate, from your equation, how many miles per gallon passenger cars will average in the years 2010, 2015, 2020, and 2030.

2010: _____          2020: _____

2015: _____          2030: _____

4.  Use your numerical analysis to write a speech for the division director. Include supporting graphs and charts.

# 25. Average Salary

## Context

sports

## Topic

nonlinear functions

## Overview

In this activity, students investigate how baseball salaries are changing over time and use that information to make predictions about future salaries.

## Objectives

Students will be able to:

- graph and interpret nonlinear functions
- derive equations from data
- use data and graphs to draw conclusions

## Materials

- one copy of the Activity 25 handout for each student
- graph paper
- graphing calculators

## Teaching Notes

- Students can work individually or in pairs for this activity.
- Minimum salary represents the least amount a Major League Baseball player may be paid.
- Many students are unsure of how to begin to construct a graph. Review graphing fundamentals with them.

- When using graphing calculators, many students have difficulty choosing appropriate settings for their graphs. Review this prior to using the activity.
- Students should have some familiarity with working with curves of best fit and with doing regressions.

## Answers

1. Answers will vary but should note that minimum salaries have increased (with the exception of '99–'01) and that average salaries have increased even more (with the exception of '01–'03).

2. Students should list years on the $x$-axis and salary amounts on the $y$-axis. Intervals should be about 1–2 on the $x$-axis and about 10,000 on the $y$-axis.

3. Answers will vary but should note to what extent the scale/intervals reflected the pattern of increase.

4. possible equation for minimum salary:
   $y = 307.12x^2 \times 1,212,601x + 1,196,931,796$
   possible equation for average salary:
   $y = e^{(.141117x - 267.6425)}$

5. Answers will vary but equation for average salary will have a larger factor.

6–7. Answers will vary depending on present year.

## Extension Activity

Have students conduct a similar investigation for other professional sports.

**64**

# 25. Average Salary

Imagine you're a college baseball player who has just been drafted by a Major League Baseball team. Before you sit down with the team's representative to work out a contract, you want to make sure that you are well informed about baseball salaries. You have conducted some research and compiled some historical information on baseball salaries. Use the information in the table to answer the questions that follow.

### Minimum and Average Player Salaries, 1967–2005

| Year | Minimum salary ($) | Average salary ($) |
|------|------|------|
| 1967 | 6,000 | 19,000 |
| 1969 | 10,000 | 24,909 |
| 1971 | 12,750 | 31,543 |
| 1973 | 15,000 | 36,566 |
| 1975 | 16,000 | 44,676 |
| 1977 | 19,000 | 76,066 |
| 1979 | 21,000 | 113,558 |
| 1981 | 32,500 | 185,651 |
| 1983 | 35,000 | 289,194 |
| 1985 | 60,000 | 371,571 |
| 1987 | 62,500 | 412,454 |
| 1989 | 68,000 | 512,084 |
| 1991 | 100,000 | 891,188 |
| 1993 | 109,000 | 1,120,254 |
| 1995 | 109,000 | 1,071,029 |
| 1997 | 150,000 | 1,383,578 |
| 1999 | 200,000 | 1,611,166 |
| 2001 | 200,000 | 2,654,403 |
| 2003 | 300,000 | 2,555,476 |
| 2005 | 316,000 | 2,632,655 |

Source: www.baseball-almanac.com

Answer the questions that follow. Then construct graphs showing the relationship among the year and the minimum and average salaries.

1. Examine the figures in the table and describe how the graphs will look.

*(continued)*

# 25. Average Salary

2. Indicate how you will label the axes of your graph and what intervals you will select for each axis. Then construct your graph.

3. Look over the graphs and assess how accurate your answer to question 2 was.

4. Write an equation to represent each line in your graph.

   minimum salary equation: _____

   average salary equation: _____

5. In what ways do the equations differ?

6. Suppose that you will spend 3 years in the minors before making your way to the major leagues. If you sign a contract at that point for the major league minimum salary level, how much would you expect to make? Explain how you arrived at that figure.

7. Imagine you have two good seasons as a major leaguer. It is time to sign a new contract, and your agent feels you should be worth at least the average league salary. What is the lowest amount you should settle for? Explain how you arrived at that figure.

# 26. A Penny Saved Is a Penny Earned

## Context

money

## Topic

nonlinear functions

## Overview

In this activity, students assume the role of an assistant branch manager at a credit union. They must devise a plan to encourage credit union members to put more money into their savings accounts.

## Objectives

Students will be able to:

- calculate compound interest

- demonstrate an understanding of the relationship among interest rates, dividends, and compounded interest schedule

## Materials

- one copy of the Activity 26 handout for each student

## Teaching Notes

- Students can work individually or in pairs for this activity.

- Students may need an explanation about the concept of compound interest prior to using the activity.

## Answers

1. Answers will vary depending on amount selected.

2. Some of the ways students could decide to increase members' contributions include paying higher dividends (make sure rates are reasonable), compounding interest more frequently (e.g., monthly), and matching deposited funds.

3. Reports will vary but should be supported with specific calculations.

## Extension Activity

Students can investigate other options for saving money in a credit union or bank, such as certificates of deposit and money market accounts.

# 26. A Penny Saved Is a Penny Earned

Imagine you have just finished reviewing the financial records at the north branch of the City Employees Federal Credit Union (CEFCU). You are concerned because you think CEFCU members are not putting enough money into their savings accounts. As a new assistant branch manager, you want to help advance your career by showing your branch manager and district supervisor that you can identify and solve problems that CEFCU faces. Identifying the problem was the easy part. Now you have to figure out a way for CEFCU to encourage members to place more money into their savings accounts. Listed in the table below are the current savings account rates and dividend payment schedules. Use this information and the formula for compound interest to devise a plan to increase members' contributions to savings.

### CEFCU Savings Account Information[1]

| Account balance | Dividend rate |
|---|---|
| $5–$500 | 3.25% |
| $501–$2500 | 3.50% |
| $2501 and above | 3.75% |

[1] Dividends are compounded and paid quarterly.

1.  As you devise your plan, calculate compound interest for at least one balance amount using the following formula:

$$A = P\left(1 + \frac{r}{n}\right)^{nt}$$

   where $A$ = the balance in the account after a certain amount of time, $P$ = the amount placed in savings, $r$ = the dividend rate (expressed as a decimal), $t$ = time in years, and $n$ = number of times interest is compounded per year.

2.  Think about the results of your calculations and the issue of insufficient deposits. List some of the ways that CEFCU could encourage members to put more money into their savings accounts. Compare your ideas with another student's.

3.  Prepare a report for the branch manager and district supervisor detailing your plan for increasing members' contributions to savings accounts. Support your plan with projections based on calculations of compound interest.

**teacher's page**

# 27. The Bounce Test

## Context

science/technology

## Topic

nonlinear functions

## Overview

In this activity, students conduct an experiment to determine the bouncing characteristics of super high-bouncing balls.

## Objectives

Students will be able to:

- graph and interpret nonlinear functions
- derive equations from data
- use data and graphs to draw conclusions

## Materials

- one copy of the Activity 27 handout for each student
- graph paper
- graphing calculators
- super high-bouncing balls, four different types per group
- data collection device, one per group (optional)

## Teaching Notes

- Students should work in small groups for this activity.
- Prior to conducting the experiment, each group should assign specific roles to each member for measuring heights,

time keeping, and recording data. You may want to use a data collection device to record bounce heights.

- Remind students that the objective is to find out not how high the balls bounce, but rather the frequency of bounces.
- Students may get confused about what they should graph. Explain that they will be graphing the relationship between bounce number and the height of the bounce.
- Many students are unsure of how to begin to construct a graph. Review graphing fundamentals with those students.
- Likewise, when they are using graphing calculators, many students have difficulty choosing appropriate settings for their graphs. Review this procedure prior to using the activity.
- Students should have some familiarity with working with curves of best fit and with doing regressions.

## Answers

1. Graphs will vary.
2. Lines and equations should be modeled by an exponential function.
3. Reports will vary.

## Extension Activity

Students can design a separate experiment to determine which balls bounce the highest.

# 27. The Bounce Test

Imagine you've just finished eight long years of college and have earned a Ph.D. in chemistry. Your first assignment as a research scientist at Acme Toy Company, home of the Amazing-Super-Bouncing Ball, is to invent a new and improved Amazing-Super-Bouncing Ball. However, before you can do that, you must become familiar with the competition. In the competitive high-bouncing ball market, Acme wants to stand out as having the ball that bounces higher and longer than all the rest. Your job is to conduct an experiment and document how the competition performs. When you've finished with your experiment, you will need to turn in a report of your findings.

**Set Up and Conduct the Experiment**

1.  Select at least four different super high-bouncing balls to test.

2.  Choose a suitable location. Measure the height from which you will drop the balls. Record the location and height below.



3.  Create a table such as the one below to record your results. The high-bouncing balls will probably bounce more than five times, so you'll need to make your table bigger. Create a separate table for each ball that you test.

### Height of Bounce

| Bounce No. | Ball Type 1 | Ball Type 2 | Ball Type 3 | Ball Type 4 |
|---|---|---|---|---|
| 1 | | | | |
| 2 | | | | |
| 3 | | | | |
| 4 | | | | |
| 5 | | | | |

### Total Bounce Time

| Ball Type | Total Bounce Time (seconds) |
|---|---|
| 1 | |
| 2 | |
| 3 | |
| 4 | |

**Analyze Your Findings**

1.  Construct a graph using the data from your tables.

2.  Find the best-fitting line for each set of data, and then write an equation to model those lines.

3.  Write a report detailing how the super high-bouncing balls in your test performed and your recommendations about how the new and improved Amazing-Super-Bouncing Ball will have to be designed.

# 28. The 2-Second Rule

## Context

travel/transportation

## Topic

nonlinear functions

## Overview

In this activity, students conduct an experiment to determine the stopping distance of cars at various speeds.

## Objectives

Students will be able to:

- graph and interpret nonlinear functions

- derive equations from data

- use data and graphs to draw conclusions

## Materials

- one copy of the Activity 28 handout for each student

- graph paper

- graphing calculators

- tape measure

- two-way radio

- car

- access to a parking lot or other safe place to conduct the experiment

## Teaching Notes

- Students can work individually, in pairs, or in small groups for most of the activity. Most likely, though, the whole class will be involved in measuring braking distances.

- Have students calculate reaction distances prior to conducting the braking distance experiment. Students may have trouble converting between units of measure, so you may want to model this calculation for the whole class.

## Setting Up and Conducting the Braking Distance Experiment

- Arrange this part of the activity prior to the Braking Distance section of the activity.

- Safety should be the number-one priority when using this activity. You will need to enlist the help of three or more adults. Only adults should operate the vehicle. Another adult should ride along as a safety observer and two-way radio operator.

- Likewise, there should be more than one adult with the students to ensure safety.

- Obey all traffic laws when conducting this experiment.

*(continued)*

# 28. The 2-Second Rule

- You may want to check with your local law enforcement agency prior to conducting the braking distance experiment.

- Choose a parking lot or other suitable location where the braking distance experiment can safely be conducted. If you are having difficulty finding a suitable location, modify the speeds tested, or travel to a more suitable location.

- Only do the experiment when roads are dry.

- Under ideal conditions, anticipate about 100 feet of braking distance for a car traveling at 40 mph.

- When braking, it is not necessary to "slam on" the brakes. Stop in a controlled manner.

- Start applying the brakes at the same location for each speed; this will make measurement of braking distances easier.

- Do not measure braking distances for speeds in excess of 40 mph. That part of the table should be derived from students' graphs and/or equations.

## Answers

### Reaction Distance

(based on 0.75-second reaction time)

| | |
|---|---|
| 15 mph: 16 ft | 45 mph: 49 ft |
| 20 mph: 22 ft | 50 mph: 55 ft |
| 25 mph: 27 ft | 55 mph: 60 ft |
| 30 mph: 33 ft | 65 mph: 71 ft |
| 35 mph: 38 ft | 75 mph: 82 ft |
| 40 mph: 44 ft | |

### Braking Distance

Answers will vary. According to the Arkansas Department of Public Safety, under ideal conditions, braking distances would be:

| | |
|---|---|
| 20 mph: 24 ft | 50 mph: 146 ft |
| 30 mph: 54 ft | 60 mph: 215 ft |
| 40 mph: 96 ft | 70 mph: 290 ft |

### Stopping Distance

5. Under ideal conditions, it would take closer to 3 seconds than 2 seconds to stop at 55 mph.

## Extension Activity

Students can research how different road conditions, such as rain and snow, affect stopping distances.

# 28. The 2-Second Rule

If you have taken a driver's education class, or if you already have your driver's license, you have probably heard of the 2-second rule. The 2-second rule simply means that you should leave a 2-second gap between your car and the car in front of you. But does the 2-second rule provide a large enough margin of safety? Let's conduct an experiment and find out.

## Stopping Distance

The *stopping distance,* or total distance it takes a car to come to a stop, is made up of two components—reaction distance and braking distance. *Reaction distance* is the distance the car travels from the time the driver realizes the need to stop the car to the time the driver steps on the brake. *Braking distance* is the distance a vehicle continues to travel once the brakes have been applied and the vehicle comes to a stop.

## Reaction Distance

Calculate the reaction distances for the speeds listed in the table below. Assume 0.75 seconds for time.

| MPH | 15 | 20 | 25 | 30 | 35 | 40 | 45 | 50 | 55 | 65 |
|-----|----|----|----|----|----|----|----|----|----|----|
| Reaction distance (ft.) | | | | | | | | | | |

## Braking Distance

Measure the braking distances for the speeds listed in the table.

| MPH | 15 | 20 | 25 | 30 | 35 | 40 |
|-----|----|----|----|----|----|----|
| Braking distance (ft.) | | | | | | |
| Stopping distance (ft.) | | | | | | |

## Stopping Distance

Calculate the stopping distance for the speeds listed in the table on the next page. Remember, stopping distance is the sum of the reaction distance and braking distance.

*(continued)*

# 28. The 2-Second Rule

| MPH | 15 | 20 | 30 | 35 | 40 |
|---|---|---|---|---|---|
| Stopping distance (ft.) | | | | | |

1. If you were to graph the data in the reaction distance, braking distance, and stopping distance tables, what would each of the graphs look like? Explain.



2. Construct a graph showing the relationship among speed, reaction distance, braking distance, and stopping distance.

3. Write an equation to model the reaction distance, braking distance, and stopping distance.

   reaction distance: _____

   braking distance: _____

   stopping distance: _____

4. Use the graphs and/or equations you created to fill in the table below, which shows the braking and stopping distances for higher speeds.

**Braking and Stopping Distances**

| MPH | 45 | 50 | 55 | 65 | 75 |
|---|---|---|---|---|---|
| Braking distance | | | | | |
| Stopping distance | | | | | |

5. Prove whether this statement is valid: "The 2-second rule provides a safe margin for speeds of 55 mph or higher."

**teacher's page**

# 29. Play Ball

## Context

sports

## Topic

miscellaneous

## Overview

In this activity, students learn about a way that baseball statisticians determine who is the best hitter at a given position.

## Objectives

Students will be able to:

- use and apply formulas

- analyze data

## Materials

- one copy of the Activity 29 handout for each student

## Teaching Notes

- Some students may need additional background information about what the various baseball statistics mean. If you are uncomfortable providing this information, have a student or coach explain what the statistics are and how they are used.

- Be aware that students sometimes make an error using the RC/25 formula by trying to cancel out the 25s when doing the final calculation for the RC/25 value.

## Answers

1. Texeira: 7.14

2. Konerko: 7.98

3. Sexson: 6.04

4. Giambi: 6.69

## Extension Activities

- Students can research other uncommon or unusual statistical measures used in baseball or other sports.

- At the end of the season, have students compare the RC/25 ratings of players who were selected for recognition (such as all-conference) with ratings of other players in the league.

- Divide the class into eight groups, and assign a baseball position to each group. Give the class statistics for your school's baseball team, and have students calculate the RC/25 ratings for players in that position.

# 29.  Play Ball

Can you identify the best hitters in baseball? According to Bill James, renowned baseball statistician, there is a simple way to do this. He invented a statistic called RC/25. RC/25 measures how many runs a line-up of 9 of the same individual would score per game. RC/25 has been widely accepted by baseball statisticians. In other words, the player with the highest RC/25 would be the best player at that particular position. Practice using the formulas for RC/25 by determining who was the best-hitting first baseman in the American League in 2006.

**RC/25 Formulas**

$$A = H + BB - CS \qquad\qquad C = AB + BB \qquad\qquad RC = \frac{AB}{C}$$

$$B = {}^*TB + 0.52SB + 0.26BB \qquad D = (AB - H + CS) \qquad RC/25 = 25\,\frac{RC}{D}$$

| Key | | |
|---|---|---|
| H = hits | BB = bases on balls (walks) | CS = caught stealing |
| SB = stolen bases | AB = at-bats | |
| *TB = total bases = [2(2B) + 3(3B) + 4(HR)] + H − [(2B) + (3B) + (HR)] | | |

To calculate RC/25, first find the values for A, B, C, and D. Then calculate the value for RC. Finally, divide RC by D, and then multiply the result by 25. This will be the player's RC/25 value.

1.  What are the RC/25 values for the following American League first basemen for the 2006 baseball season? Rank these players and list the results in the table below.

| PLAYER | H | 2B | 3B | HR | BB | SB | CS | AB |
|---|---|---|---|---|---|---|---|---|
| Mark Texeira | 177 | 45 | 1 | 33 | 89 | 2 | 0 | 628 |
| Paul Konerko | 177 | 30 | 0 | 35 | 60 | 1 | 0 | 566 |
| Richie Sexson | 156 | 40 | 0 | 34 | 64 | 1 | 1 | 591 |
| Jason Giambi | 113 | 25 | 0 | 37 | 110 | 2 | 0 | 496 |

Source: www.sportsline.com

| Rank | Player | RC/25 |
|---|---|---|
| 1 | | |
| 2 | | |
| 3 | | |
| 4 | | |

*Real-Life Math: Algebra*

# 30. Which Mortgage?

## Context

money

## Topic

miscellaneous

## Overview

In this activity, students select houses they would like to buy and evaluate different types of mortgage loans for those homes.

## Objectives

Students will be able to:

- analyze data

- use formulas to appraise available information and make decisions

## Materials

- one copy of the Activity 30 handout for each student

- newspapers, other publications, or online resources that list homes for sale

## Teaching Notes

- Students can work individually, in pairs, or in small groups for this activity.

- Students can select any houses they want for this activity.

- You may want to use graphing calculators with business applications for this activity.

## Answers

Answers will vary depending on the houses students select. However, in deciding between the loans, students should make a clear case for the type of loan they choose.

## Extension Activities

- Students can make comparisons with other types of loans, such as 15-year conventional fixed-rate loans.

- Have students calculate total payments and determine how much interest is paid during the life of the loan.

# 30. Which Mortgage?

Someday you may want to buy a house, and most likely you will have to get a mortgage loan. Not too long ago, getting a mortgage loan was a simple decision. But things are very different today. Now there are many different types of loans to choose from. For instance, you can get a conventional fixed-rate loan for 15 years, a conventional fixed-rate loan for 30 years, an adjustable-rate loan, a 7-year balloon jumbo loan, and many others. To add to the confusion, there are different types of loans within each loan category. Find out more about mortgage loans by completing the activity below.

1.  Look through the newspaper or another publication or visit an Internet site that lists homes for sale. Select three houses that you might like to buy. List the prices below.

    a. _____     b. _____     c. _____

2.  Lenders offer loans with terms that differ based on interest rates and "points." A point is a fee that equals 1% of the loan amount and must be paid upfront. Lenders typically offer loans of the same type that differ based on the number of points and interest rates. To compare similar loans, you must consider interest rates and upfront costs such as points. Suppose a lender offered 30-year conventional loans with the following conditions:

| Loan | Annual interest rate | Points |
|------|---------------------|--------|
| Loan A | 6.25% | 4.00 |
| Loan B | 6.50% | 2.75 |
| Loan C | 6.75% | 1.75 |
| Loan D | 7.25% | 0.00 |

To calculate monthly payments, use the given formula:

$$m = \frac{A(\frac{r}{12})(1 + \frac{r}{12})^n}{(1 + \frac{r}{12})^n - 1}$$

where $m$ = the monthly payment, $A$ = the amount of the loan, $r$ = the annual interest rate (expressed as a decimal), and $n$ = the number of months of the loan.

Appraise the different loans for the houses you selected. Choose the loan that would be the best choice for you. Explain how you made your selection.

**teacher's page**

# 31. Asphyxia

## Context

science/technology

## Topic

miscellaneous

## Overview

In this activity, students learn about breath-hold diving and partial pressure of gases.

## Objectives

Students will be able to:

- graph and interpret functions

- use data and graphs to draw conclusions

## Materials

- one copy of the Activity 31 handout for each student

- stopwatches or wristwatches with a stopwatch function (one per pair of students)

## Teaching Notes

- Students should work in pairs for this activity.

- This lesson can be used in conjunction with a science class that is studying gas laws.

- Before beginning, check if students have asthma or other medical conditions that would prevent them from completing the physical portion of the activity.

- Some students may want to do the experiment in a pool. Caution them that hyperventilating or breathing rapidly prior to holding your breath under water is very dangerous and can lead to shallow-water blackout and even death.

## Answers

1. Breakpoint is at about 50 $ppO_2$ and 50 $ppCO_2$.

2–5. Answers will vary.

## Extension Activity

Collect the breath-holding times for the entire class and have students calculate class averages.

# 31. Asphyxia

Imagine that you are standing next to a swimming pool. As you dive into the water, you take a deep breath and try to swim all the way across the pool underwater. But before you make it to the other side of the pool the urge to breathe becomes overwhelming, and you have to rise to the surface and get some air. Do you know why? According to the U.S. Navy Dive Manual, when breathing stops, the oxygen ($O_2$) level in your body falls as oxygen is used by tissues in the body. As this is happening, the carbon dioxide ($CO_2$) level in your blood rises as tissues produce the gas. The rising carbon dioxide levels stimulate you to breathe by producing the sensation of air hunger. These changes occur more rapidly as your level of activity increases. Scientists measure these changes in oxygen and carbon dioxide levels using a concept known as partial pressure of gases. The relationship between the partial pressure of oxygen ($ppO_2$) and the partial pressure of carbon dioxide ($ppCO_2$) determines when it becomes necessary to breathe.

1.  The following table lists the oxygen and carbon dioxide partial pressures found in a person's lungs during a typical shallow-water breath-hold dive.

| Breath-hold duration (seconds) | $ppCO_2$ (mmHg) | $ppO_2$ (mmHg) |
| --- | --- | --- |
| Start | 38 | 100 |
| 10 | 43 | 90 |
| 20 | 48 | 80 |
| 30 | 49 | 70 |
| 40 | 50 | 60 |

The point at which a diver needs to breathe (breakpoint) is when the partial pressures of the oxygen and carbon dioxide equal each other. Construct a graph that shows the relationship between the gases, and then determine the breakpoint for this dive.

partial pressures of $CO_2$ and $O_2$ at breakpoint: _____

2.  Now try this experiment: While you are sitting still in your chair, take a deep breath and hold it for as long as you can (no cheating allowed). As you're doing this, have your partner time how long it takes before you have to breathe. Then switch roles and repeat the experiment. List your results below.

name and time: _____

name and time: _____

3.  If you were to do the same experiment while exercising, how do you think your time would change?

*(continued)*

# 31. Asphyxia

4. Now try the same experiment while you're working out. Take a deep breath and hold it for as long as you can (no cheating allowed here either). This time, perform a simple exercise such as jumping jacks or running in place. Again, as you're doing this, have your partner time how long it takes before you have to breathe. Then switch roles and repeat the experiment. List your results below.

   name and time: _____

   name and time: _____

5. Construct a table that could represent what your $ppCO_2$ and $ppO_2$ amounts might have measured during the two experiments.

| Breath-hold duration (seconds) | $ppCO_2$ (mmHg) | $ppO_2$ (mmHg) |
|---|---|---|
| start | | |
| 10 | | |
| 20 | | |
| 30 | | |
| 40 | | |

| Breath-hold duration (seconds) | $ppCO_2$ (mmHg) | $ppO_2$ (mmHg) |
|---|---|---|
| start | | |
| 10 | | |
| 20 | | |
| 30 | | |
| 40 | | |

         *Real-Life Math: Algebra*

# 32. Rules of the Sea

## Context

travel/transportation

## Topic

miscellaneous

## Overview

In this activity, students learn about rules mariners use to estimate distance traveled.

## Objectives

Students will be able to:

- solve problems using the Rule of 3 and the 6-Minute Rule

## Materials

- one copy of the Activity 32 handout for each student

## Teaching Notes

- Students should work individually on this activity.

- You and your students shouldn't need any prior nautical background knowledge to understand and solve the problems in the activity.

- Both the Rule of 3 and the 6-Minute Rule are specialized applications of the distance, rate, time formula.

- The rules are intended to be solved mentally. Introduce the activity by solving a problem using one of the rules while explaining your line of thinking.

- Explain to students that distances at sea are measured using nautical miles, which are slightly longer than statute miles. Also, speeds are measured as knots, which are slightly faster than mph.

## Answers

1. 1500 yards

2. $15 \times \dfrac{2000}{60} \times 3 = 1500$ yards

3. Answers will vary but should include an example (not a multiple of 3) that doesn't work.

4. 2 nautical miles

5. 24 minutes

6. Answers will vary but should describe the common concept of knots/nautical miles relating to minutes in a predictable way.

## Extension Activity

Have students set up and solve other problems using these rules.

# 32.  Rules of the Sea

### The Rule of 3

The Rule of 3 is a mental calculation that mariners use to estimate how far they will travel in 3 minutes. For example, if your boat is traveling at a speed of 3 knots, to calculate how far you'll travel (in yards) in 3 minutes, you simply add two zeroes to the speed. So in this case, at a speed of 3 knots you would travel 300 yards. If your speed was 9 knots, you would travel 900 yards in 3 minutes. Now try solving the following problem.

1. If you are on a boat traveling at a speed of 15 knots, how far would you travel in 3 minutes?

2. Verify the accuracy of the Rule of 3 by calculating the actual distance (in yards) you would travel in 3 minutes at a speed of 15 knots. A knot is based on a nautical mile, which is equal to 2000 yards (a mile on land, or statute mile, is equal to about 1757 yards).

3. Mariners know that the Rule of 3 only works for speeds that are multiples of 3 (for example, 6 knots, 9 knots, 12 knots, and so forth). Set up a problem that proves that this statement is correct, and explain why the Rule of 3 cannot be used for speeds that are not multiples of 3.

### The 6-Minute Rule

The 6-Minute Rule is another mental math relationship that mariners use to estimate distance traveled. This rule states that the distance a boat covers in 6 minutes is equal to $\frac{1}{10}$ its speed. For example, a boat traveling at 5 knots covers 0.5 nautical miles in 6 minutes, or 3 nautical miles in 36 minutes. Use the 6-Minute Rule to answer the questions that follow.

4. How far would a boat traveling at a speed of 20 knots travel in 6 minutes?

5. How many minutes would it take that same boat, traveling at a speed of 20 knots, to cover 8 nautical miles?

6. Describe the similarities between the 6-Minute Rule and the Rule of 3.